MY MONEY MYSELF

MY MONEY MYSELF

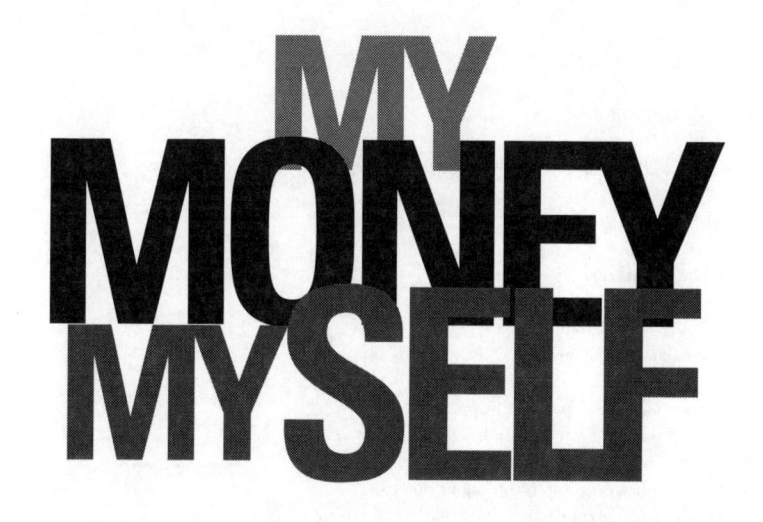

Hands-on, basic financial planning for women of all ages

Anne Ingram & Peggy O'Donnell

CHOICEBOOKS

A CHOICE BOOK

Copyright © Anne Ingram and Peggy O'Donnell 2002

First published in 2002 by
CHOICE Books
Australian Consumers' Association
57 Carrington Road
Marrickville NSW 2204 Australia
http://www.choice.com.au

All rights reserved. No part of this publication
may be reproduced, stored in a retrieval system or
transmitted in any form or by any means, electronic,
mechanical, photocopying, recording or otherwise,
without the prior permission of the publisher in writing.
No part of this publication may be used in any form of
advertising, sales promotion or publicity.

National Library of Australia
Cataloguing-in-publication data

> Ingram, Anne Bower.
> My money myself : hands-on, basic financial planning for
> women of all ages.
>
> Includes index.
> ISBN 0 947277 96 X.
>
> 1. Finance, Personal. 2. Women - Finance, Personal. I.
> O'Donnell, Peggy. II. Title.

332.024042

ISBN 0 947277 96 X

Edited by Gillian Gillet
Designed and typeset by Anna Warren, Warren Ventures Pty Ltd
Cover design by Anna Warren, Warren Ventures Pty Ltd
Cover photograph © Lynn Scott
Illustration by Anna Warren, Warren Ventures Pty Ltd

Printed in Australia by Griffin Press

For Lynn
a special daughter and a special friend

ACKNOWLEDGEMENTS

The authors would like to thank Kate Beddoe who read the manuscript, and special thanks to the many women who shared their money 'experiences' with us.

DISCLAIMER

The authors and the publisher have made every effort to ensure that the information in this book is accurate and current at the time of publication and is given in good faith. No warranty of accuracy or reliability is given and the authors and the publisher cannot be held responsible for any errors or omissions. They strongly recommend that a professional adviser be consulted before any investment decisions are made.

CONTENTS

• • •

	INTRODUCTION	ix
1.	THE THREE STAGES OF MONEY MANAGEMENT	13
2.	STARTING POINT	21
3.	CREDIT: USES AND ABUSES	29
4.	BANKING BASICS	39
5.	ON YOUR WAY	49
6.	INVESTMENT OPTIONS	65
7.	SHARES	77
8.	REAL ESTATE	95
9.	YOUR OWN BUSINESS	115
10.	TAXING MATTERS	127
11.	CUTTING COSTS	141
12.	BUYING ALONE	149
13.	INSURANCE, SUPER AND PENSIONS	155
14.	FUN MONEY	167
	CONTACTS	175
	GLOSSARY	182
	INDEX	189

INTRODUCTION

• • •

> Let the bloodhounds of money beware.
> Mary Elizabeth Lease

We all need and want money. We all dream about what we would do if only we had that little bit extra. The needs and wants are different for every one of us and they change as we change. We must develop our own financial plans and be prepared to revise and change them continuously — what we need and want at 20 will change by 30 and be entirely unrelated at 50 and 70.

Research seems to be pointing to a future that is in women's favour. Certainly we are doing well in the education field where girls now have the opportunity to perform equally with the boys, outperforming them in many subjects. In the workplace we are slowly making our mark, more of us are breaking that glass ceiling and reaching the boardroom. Many women are now owners of their own successful companies in the international market.

For years Anne and Peggy have been attending free seminars given by investment companies and the Australian Stock Exchange, as well as seeking advice from financial advisers in the various banks. Time and time again, however, we have come away with the feeling that no one has really understood our particular needs at our different ages, and that everything must be assessed and updated on a regular basis.

My Money, Myself is for women. It was written by two women who had to get out there and make their money work or go under. It was a steep learning curve, partly because, for too long we had been brain-washed into thinking that managing money is men's business.

This is a book for women of all ages and incomes. It is for women who prefer to be in charge, who want to take control of their money and plan where they are heading. There are hundreds of books available written by experts. This one is different. It has been designed as a simple introduction for the many women with no experience of managing their own finances, who now want to learn and take charge. It is a book to set them on that road.

This is the third book we have written about money. It was not a subject we ever intended writing about and each book has been written as the result of outside influences. The first, for children aged eight to twelve, was a knee-jerk reaction, to a request for ice cream from Peggy's granddaughters, aged five and six. When told afternoon tea was waiting at home and we had no change, their solution was simple: 'Put it on card, Grandma'. Obviously it was time they learned about money.

The second book, for teenagers, was written in answer to a plea from our publisher whose teenagers were keeping him poor. To them money came from parents and the government. Why study, work or save when there was always someone else who would look after you?

My Money, Myself has been written for our many friends and acquaintances who have purchased and read our previous books for children and wanted us to write one for them — in the same simple language — explaining how we had managed to educate our children, own our own home and car, build a portfolio of shares, buy investment properties and travel extensively each year, even though we had both left school at 15 and were both divorced — Anne at 39 and Peggy at 50.

Because of the thirteen-year difference in our ages, our financial needs, wants, plans and outlooks have been different. We both learned about managing money early in our lives. Anne took over the family affairs when she was 23, after her father died suddenly. Peggy ran a small farm and coped with three young children while her husband spent long periods at sea. We both moved to Sydney and have lived in the same block of townhouses since the early 1970s. We quickly became friends when we took over the running of the body corporate — the committee were into spending with no funds in hand, involving the raising of special levies for us all. As there were a number of women in our block struggling to bring up and educate children alone, the women elected women and managed to bring the affairs of the body corporate into credit within two years.

We are not financial experts but we have learned that making money work is not hard. Education through research is the key. By sharing the things we have learned and the mistakes we have made over the years, we may be able to help other women save time, money and heartache, and create the confidence to try. All of us have a right to use our own money to do with as we please, to give us our independence and security and the joy and fun of spending the profits.

> Money is like a spirited horse.
> One must know how to ride it.
> *Ferdinand Lundberg*

1. THE THREE STAGES OF MONEY MANAGEMENT

• • •

Money is like muck, not good except it be spread.
Francis Bacon

Women are living longer than their grandmothers did. If we can get past the danger years and reach 65, our life expectancy extends to 85, and if we make it to 85 we can look forward to another seven or eight years. Men's life expectancy is at least five years shorter than women's, yet because we are paid less than men, on average, our superannuation is smaller, and has to stretch further, especially if we have given up work to raise a family.

Childbearing and rearing means that many women will spend less time in full-time paid employment than their male partner, who will have around 40 years to build up his investments and his super. A woman who wants to retire free of money worries without depending entirely on a pension has no alternative but to learn how to make her smaller income grow faster. Women make up 51 per cent of the population but we certainly don't own 51 per cent of the wealth. It's time to change that.

The traditional partnership of working husband and housekeeping wife is no longer the norm. Two incomes have become necessary for a family to stay afloat and enjoy a few extra comforts. Whether you are a traditional or a working partner you need to take an active part in managing the money. If you are one of the many women who live alone, it is vital to be in control of your money, not just to survive but to enjoy a full, secure life.

Money management — making it work and grow — can be divided into three key stages of your life, and each stage sub-divides and overlaps. Throughout the book we refer to these stages to highlight the options available and to help you clarify your thoughts as you plan your diversified and growing financial portfolio.

1. Spending Years	2. Growth Years	3. Freedom Years
Buy, Hold & Buy, Buy	Buy & Hold for 10	Buy & Sell as needed
16 – 36	36 – 56	56 +

1. SPENDING YEARS

Your first pay-packet, money of your own to do with as you please — surely one of the great moments in life! The choices seem unlimited — clothes, car, parties, a flat of your own, maybe a higher degree, travel, freedom! Everything seems possible at first, but it doesn't take many months to realise that freedom has a price and a responsibility, especially if the pay-packet does not last from one week to the next.

A budget is essential from the first payday. Without it, you have no idea of how you will manage to pay rent, buy food and clothes and, maybe, pay off and run a car. You also need to budget for entertainment (relaxation is essential, life is for living) and save something for that step into the investment world. Be realistic, live within your budget. Stay in the black and recognise the difference between your 'needs' — what you need to survive — and your 'wants' — luxuries of life that are not essential. Don't set yourself impossible goals, and be patient about saving — it's the length of time your money stays in, not how much you invest, that pays the dividends.

This is the best time in your life to build a share portfolio — you have youth on your side. Risks can be taken but don't expect to make your fortune in one killing. You might consider risks such as shares in ventures like the dot.com start-ups, but remember 2001 when so many of these fantastic boomers rocketed so high, virtually overnight. Some survived but others went to the wall. You can recoup at least some of your losses, you have time on your side, and you'll learn a lot on the way.

Focus on real estate as your next target. Start small. Get your single pad up and running. Pay it off before you take kids and partners aboard and hold on to it — don't be talked into selling it. Use it as a security for the next purchase but keep it in your own name and build on it. Independent money is essential for everyone.

This is the time to become part of the superannuation world. You will be building a great asset and even if you take time out to travel or have a family, your super will keep growing. The sooner you start your super, the bigger the money will become. A good way to establish long-term financial independence is to invest 10 per cent of your income into extra super or a 'no touch' growth investment — the 10 per cent rule. Then, if you still have spare money, put it into short-term investments for that trip you are planning.

The time may come when you decide to set up with a partner, or maybe start a family, together or alone. Now money management becomes vital and time spent on research and planning is never wasted. Reassess your budget, always allowing for that 10 per cent savings rule.

> **Fiona** When I finished university and went looking for my first job, I decided to leave home and set up in a flat with my best friend. The freedom lasted six months. Without a regular income the expenses were too much so I moved back home. Now I have a full-time job and a car which I'm paying off. I'm able to meet all my other expenses, including my health insurance and I'm saving to travel, paying a token rent and building up some capital. My plan is to invest in shares, keeping them 'no touch', so that when I return from overseas I'll have some ready money of my own.
>
> I have *no* credit cards — I believe that if you haven't got the cash you can't have it or don't need it. I have

watched too many of my friends run up big debts on their cards and end up in trouble. I realise the advantages of using plastic when I travel and intend getting my first card before I leave Australia. I learned the basics about money management when I had to look after my parents' affairs while they were working overseas for two years.

2. GROWTH YEARS

At this stage your money grows and so do the demands on it. If you have children, they will have become more expensive as they move on through school and into higher education. You may also have an older relative to take into your budget considerations. Your interests will have changed and expanded and it's time to reassess your budget and long-term investment plans. Keep the 10 per cent rule in mind.

Wise investments made in the spending years will pay off now. If you did nothing in those years, it's time to get started. Retirement will come sooner than you think, so if you want to enjoy your freedom years in reasonable comfort, to plan for them now.

As always, research is essential and it's wise to seek advice from an expert. These are your peak earning years and how you manage your income will influence your future financial well-being, so don't waste them! Spare a thought for your grandchildren — they are the ones who will be struggling to pay for the ever-increasing 'grey' population.

Bits & Bytes
Opportunity knocks only once. Temptation keeps ringing the doorbell. Seize the opportunity and then you can welcome temptation.

The growth years have a lot going for them. You have made your choices and have settled into your life. You may have the choice of returning to full-time work as family responsibilities decrease. Your superannuation should now look as if it might be useful later on. If you receive an inheritance, don't rush out and blow it on a whim, make it work for something bigger. Long-service leave may also be due and the end of the mortgage should be well in sight. This is an excellent time to build both a share and a property portfolio, using the equity in your home as an investment to get you started. If you began doing this in your spending years you may well have two or three properties by now.

In the later years of this stage you need to keep a closer eye on your financial plan and work it to your advantage as the freedom years loom closer — they sneak up on us much faster than we want or expect.

Bits & Bytes
What a life! This is roughly how we spend it:

6 years are spent eating	11 years working
5 years to wash and dress	3 years learning
8 years of fun	6 years walking
3 years reading	3 years talking
24 years sleeping!	

3. FREEDOM YEARS

If you've achieved your career goals, now is the time to enjoy all those things you'd put on hold. Many career women have secured their retirement packages and added to their super and portfolios but even the best of retirement plans need to be assessed, reworked and supplemented. Budgets have become a priority as most of us are on fixed incomes and are 'captive' taxpayers. Your money may have to last another 25 years so this is not the time to sit back and watch the soapies. Set your goals and go for them — with careful planning, these can be the best years of your life.

Whether or not you have taken the career path, you still have a lot of living to do, so keep your eye on your investments. Spend your children's inheritance — if you don't, they will! If the nest is empty, downsize the house. Make the move and look forward to less housework, an intimate garden and more time for freedom — maybe even that cruise on the QEII?

Don't ease up on money management. If you are only now starting down the investment road, reappraise your budget and decide what you want your money to do for you, then get on with your research and seek expert advice. Decide if you want a managed investment, such as rolling over your super into an allocated pension fund, buying units in managed trusts or regular income funds. You may prefer to do as we do and look after your own finances. You have the time now and it's a fascinating world, even for a cautious player.

If you have already established your portfolio, your long-term investments will be maturing in these years, so all you need now is to balance your living expenses with investments that will bring in the necessary cash. One way to do this is to sell any non-performing assets and make a capital loss, spending this injection of capital as needed. You can carry forward the loss until it's time to sell assets that have increased in value, and reap the tax advantage: the retained capital loss will offset the gain, giving you a further injection of cash and reducing the tax slug.

The pension is a minefield of regulations, restrictions on assets with deeming and income tests. Everyone wants a pension but no-one should count on qualifying. It is becoming more and more important to plan your own retirement, and more difficult to judge how much you need for a comfortable life.

Hopefully, you sought expert advice in the growth years and put sound financial plans in place rather than declaring, 'I'm never going to retire'. The pension is not the safety net it's cracked up to be. For a single person, it amounts to about a quarter of the average wage, so self-help is safer and more reliable.

Superannuation, since it became compulsory, is definitely a step forward. However, it too is another minefield and its rules have changed so many times that it has become impossible to forecast

THE THREE STAGES OF MONEY MANAGEMENT

individual benefits. It has spawned a whole raft of experts. Consult one! This is the best advice we can give.

There are schemes to help you if your only asset is your home and want to stay living in it. This is a 'sale-lease-back' arrangement, whereby you sell a percentage, usually 50, of the equity in your home. You continue to live there, paying all the ongoing costs like rates, insurance and maintenance. When you have to move, or have died, the investor who has purchased a share in the house is paid the equity (not the actual cash advanced) he or she owns in the present value of the house, when this is sold. The investor is banking on realising a capital gain in the future. However, this scheme needs very careful consideration. For one thing, it can affect your pension entitlements. It may be better to take out a mortgage on the house. We strongly recommend seeking advice.

Health insurance is more necessary now. Make sure you and any dependants are fully covered for both short-term and long-term care. The Commonwealth Seniors Health Card is tied to gross income. This benefit is worth investigating.

All the statistics we read show that by retirement age:

- About 20 per cent will still be working, not because they want to but to sustain a reasonable lifestyle.
- About 5 per cent will have accumulated enough to be comfortable.
- About 1 per cent will be able to do exactly what they want — travel, buy new cars, clothes and homes and even help their children. Be a 1 per center.

Bits & Bytes

Along the road to financial freedom do *not* neglect your family and friends. Money is only important for what it can buy. That's what this book is about.

2. STARTING POINT

• • •

Get up early, work hard, find oil.
John Paul Getty Jnr.

To become a millionaire takes time and effort, though to find oil in the backyard would speed up the process. This book is not going to show you how to 'get rich quick'. Schemes such as systems to win the lottery or break the bank at the casino take advantage of our desire for instant wealth. We are all guilty of dreaming about winning the lottery, but winning money or inheriting it does not automatically mean all our problems are solved. If we don't know how to manage our money, then no matter what we win or inherit, we'll probably end up losing it all. A survey in a British newspaper, taken over the last ten years, has shown that most winners of large games of chance have blown the lot and only about 1 per cent are still wealthy after a couple of years!

Bits & Bytes
In 1966, when Australia converted to decimal currency, we had instant millionaires: suddenly one pound became two dollars and the paupers with just 500,000 pounds were worth $1,000,000.

Having a huge income does not necessarily guarantee wealth, just as having a low salary does not have to mean you will stay on the breadline all your life. It's not how much you earn, but how you work the money you earn — work it hard! We all take the time to plan our wardrobe, our holidays and our careers but how many of us spend the time planning how to make our money grow? We need to know how much we can expect our investments to earn before we can have that wardrobe or holiday.

In our world of fantastic plastic, anyone can look wealthy as they seek to impress with their clothes, cars and eating habits. In actual fact, they may own nothing — everything is on credit and the bubble can burst with just one slip. These are the people who will always be 'poor'. They use money on unnecessary disposable items, not on assets that will increase in value. The reverse side to this coin is the people who will always be 'wealthy'. They are the ones who put their money into investments that increase in value over the years — money market, shares and real estate.

Bits & Bytes
It will take you about 36 years to reach $1,000,000 if you invest $5,000 per year at 8 per cent and leave it compounding each year with no expenses taken out.

The problem with money is that it never stays around for long. It drops in for a quick cuppa and disappears out the door just when you want to get down to a serious discussion. If you're lucky it will stay overnight but next morning it will be gone. You shouldn't have had that night out with the girls, certainly not when your credit card has reached threatening levels. It's not just money that needs managing — it's you. Whatever stage in your life you have reached and whatever your goals may be, you can achieve them all by taking control of your money, yourself.

You don't need thousands to start. The principles of making money work are the same whether you have $100, $1,000 or that illusive million. Although you can't build a balanced portfolio with $100 you can still make a start.

When investment people talk about planning a balanced portfolio, what they really mean is building a spread of income and growth investments, ranging from all aspects of the share market to real estate (commercial and residential) as well as the money market. This spread is aimed at protecting the investor against inflation and or a sudden rise or fall in the investment world. If you spread your investments it is unlikely that they will all rise or fall at the same time or at the same rate.

When to start? How to start? These are the questions we are most frequently asked about managing money. It all comes down to the old donkey and carrot syndrome — everyone needs a goal to keep them going. It must be a goal that is worth working towards and making sacrifices for, such as a deposit for a home, a car, an overseas trip. Set a deadline but don't make it impossible or you'll give up.

WHEN TO START

There is no question about it — you start now! Age has nothing to do with it. Over the years we have watched too many women friends battling to keep ahead of their mortgage repayments, struggling with the incredible costs of teenagers, or worrying how to survive if retrenched or left alone. Very few have had either the time or the energy to think about the future, especially their retirement.

Nowadays you cannot afford to push retirement to the back of your mind in the hope that it is either too far down the track to worry about (the spending years), or that it's still a few years off yet and you're too busy anyway (the growth years), or that it's too late (the freedom years).

The age pension no longer provides the safety net it used to. As the population ages and the birthrate falls, the time is fast approaching when the many will have to be supported by the few. This is creating a problem that the Government has begun to address, in part, with the compulsory Superannuation Guarantee (SG). Even so, you don't have to be Einstein to work out that it is vital to set up your own retirement money to enjoy and live your freedom years to the full.

If you retire at 65 you can look forward to at least another 25 years. That's a third of your life, longer if you retire earlier and if you hope to live on the money you saved and invested during your working life (the previous third-and-a-bit years). It's a sobering thought. Your money management must start now!

HOW TO START

Research, research, research.

Research gives us knowledge, which you can turn into expertise. Then you gain the confidence to take the necessary control to make money work and grow.

Education gained by research has always been our starting-point. We read the daily newspaper and not just the money section. Much of the news has a bearing on the money market. Money programs on television, radio and the Internet are becoming a more popular and useful information source. Plenty of free brochures are made available at financial institutions and free seminars are always being held somewhere. Attend as many as you can manage, summarise the information you gather and list some questions for the next one.

Never be bamboozled into handing over your money before you are ready. Have faith in yourself and your research.

The more knowledge you gain, the more confident you will be in your own ability. Investment advisers acquire their knowledge in much the same way you do, but perhaps with a more specific focus: putting your money into their own investment field. The financial world is constantly changing. Keep reading, even after you make that first million.

Never be vague about your money, always make time to research and plan. It's your money, so be responsible with it.

Clarifying an investment strategy is the most important step to take in your financial planning. Too often we abandon long-term plans for the quick fix. Be wary of fashionable trends and concurrent on your long-term goals. Investing well is hard work, but once you have learnt the principles and overcome the intimidation of the money world, it comes naturally and is stimulating and exciting. Make the time to take stock of your finances. Begin by listing all assets and liabilities and draw up a budget — or, preferably, a profit and loss statement. Now you can see which investment is not performing, where you are being extravagant and how you can correct things.

HOW MUCH ARE YOU WORTH?

First, draw up a personal balance sheet to establish your net worth — your assets less your liabilities. This can be a surprise if you seldom take the time to look at your assets and liabilities. A personal stocktake of your financial standing should be updated once a year. By comparing each year's report you can identify the weak links in your portfolio and take the appropriate action. This stocktake reveals how much you could raise if you sold now. This statement is different to your budget (your daily ins and outs) and you need it to identify both your strengths and weaknesses to plan your financial growth.

Following the accepted rules of bookkeeping, list your assets and liabilities: debits on the left and credits on the right. It is important to give real values to assets. Try to judge what you would get for them if you disposed of them now. Don't inflate their value because this can lead to foolish decisions.

Assets can be real or intangible. Real assets include property: the house or land you own or are paying off, collectables such as paintings or jewellery, furniture and cars. Intangible assets include things such as bonds, superannuation and shares. Liabilities include mortgage or rent, car loans, credit card debts, hire purchase or any other loans you might have taken out.

Some assets are diminishing assets — they do not grow but lose value with both time and use. Your furniture and car (unless they are collector's pieces) fit into this category. Your home, unless you are downsizing or upgrading, should keep pace with the market. If you are simply changing houses, you are buying and selling on the same market, so it does not matter if the market is high or low. Equity in your home is a fantastic asset to be used as security for further investments — and property is one of the best.

Bits & Bytes
Investment properties and shares can provide a steady income and they can be sold when you need cash. Your home, on the other hand, will not give you an income. One way to make a profit from it is to downgrade it to something cheaper. It is not a cash asset — it's a lifestyle asset.

A car is an essential part of today's environment. It is counted as an asset, but is expensive to purchase and to run. From the moment you drive it out of the showroom it depreciates in value, unless it is a Ferrari or a Rolls Royce. A vintage car does increase in value with time. These can be fun but keep your budget in debit — a form of compulsory saving if you are buying and selling.

Australians are apathetic when it comes to saving. For most of us, though, saving is the only way to build assets. Take it seriously, but don't be deluded into thinking that the small amount we are putting aside for our old age will be enough. We can only look forward to our retirement if we make the most of our assets.

BUDGETS

> Annual income twenty pounds,
> annual expenditure nineteen nineteen six, result happiness.
> Annual income twenty pounds,
> annual expenditure twenty pounds ought and six,
> result misery.
> *Mr Micawber in Charles Dickens'*
> *David Copperfield*

The next step is to assess your income and expenses — in other words, get a budget up and running. If you don't know where you are, you can't know where you're heading. Your budget is the backbone of your financial plans. If it is accurate you can see at a glance where your money is coming from and going to. Once it is under control you can plan your short-term and long-term goals with confidence.

Make your budget fit your salary and your pay period and take care to review it regularly. Be realistic — don't make it so tight that you can't possibly stick to it. Be flexible but disciplined and allow for the unexpected. Financial advisers recommend keeping at least three month's income readily accessible as an emergency fund to cover things like the fridge breaking down or an unexpected illness.

> **Wendy** For the first few months after I began working I found I was rushing out, spending like mad and having a ball. I was paid monthly and discovered that at the end of the first two weeks there was nothing left to live on for the last two. My father stepped in and helped me draw up a budget which I am now sticking to. I have set myself a goal of investing $1,000 in something 'high-risk and large growth' but I intend to seek help from an adviser on the best options. I believe that at my age I can afford to try a high-risk investment as I have age and earning capacity on my side to recover if it all goes wrong.
>
> I am living at home at present. Like many of my friends I would love to have a pad of my own, but rents and ongoing costs are helping to keep young adults at home much longer these days. One of my friends, plus her four sisters, now live at home. I almost have the money for my first step into the investment world. My next goal is a flat, then travel, and for this I plan to have enough money to avoid the backpacking grind.

One of the main reasons why your savings never seem to grow is that they are forgotten when you budget. Saving 10 per cent per year of your net income should be the key to establishing financial independence. Try to make this a top priority when allocating expenses.

We buy a 13-column money book and run it in accordance with the financial year (1 July to 30 June), leaving space to add or subtract items as needed.

3. CREDIT: USAGES AND ABUSES

• • •

Neither a borrower, nor a lender be;
For a loan oft loses both itself and friend,
And borrowing dulls the edge of husbandry.
Shakespeare Hamlet Act I s. iii

Credit, in the monetary sense, has at least two meanings. First, it means the money a bank or lender makes available to a client in excess of any deposit held. Second, it denotes the positive balance in an account. Debit, in the monetary sense, acknowledges that a sum of money is owing. It also indicates an excess of liabilities over assets or expenditure over revenue. In short, it is better to be 'in the black' (in credit) than it is to be 'in the red' (in debit).

When borrowing is done sensibly it can increase your money base and make that elusive million a more achievable goal. When you ask for credit you are saying: 'Lend me this sum and I will repay it at an agreed rate and at an agreed time'.

The cost of borrowing must be built into your budget. The lender is there to make money — you get nothing for nothing. The interval of time between each repayment is an essential element of your budget: can you meet your debt, particularly with home mortgages? Do your homework before signing any loan agreement. Only since the 1980s have women been on an equal footing with men when it comes to the granting of credit.

Barbara About 20 years ago, when I decided to expand my business from home to shop, the bank refused to back me. The only way I could raise a loan was to have my husband guarantee me. What made it so frustrating was the fact that I had been running a very successful business from home, I had an established client base, no debts, stock and a good cash flow.

There are many avenues for obtaining a loan. Banks spring to mind as the first option. A small personal loan is usually available to customers whom the bank considers able to repay. Occasionally, the bank doesn't request securities, but appraises your banking record — that is, your credit record, income and expenses.

Another choice is an overdraft — the ability to withdraw an amount of money in excess of the credit in your account. This needs a secure base. Terms can be fixed or floating. Floating terms give you the flexibility to put and take as necessary, paying interest only on the amount in debit. Businesses use overdrafts to keep the cash flowing when large accounts need to be paid and the income rate is slow. There are many financial institutions in the loans business. Shop around for good terms and financially sound companies.

Credit insurance is available and we recommend it because it covers you if you are suddenly unable to meet your repayments due to sickness, retrenchment or other unforeseen circumstances. A lender usually offers credit insurance, but you don't have to accept — check out the other options.

The availability of easy credit makes for easy living, but the number of people over-extending themselves is growing every day. Handle your finances and your debts sensibly, don't keep on spending until the debt collectors are knocking at the door. Letting the convenience of credit lead us into unsustainable debt is a danger. Make sure you can service all your borrowings.

Use credit constructively — only borrow for growth assets if possible. Consumer goods such as clothing, furniture or whitegoods have a built-in obsolescence and though we need them, they will not increase our wealth in the long run. Borrowing costs: you will need to pay interest and all lenders charge either a fee or a higher interest rate to service your loan. Try to amalgamate your debts into the smallest spread possible. For example, four credit cards cost more than two and four are harder to keep track of than two. The fewer cards you have the more likely you are to stay within your budget.

CREDIT CARDS

Credit cards, debit cards, store cards and stored value cards (SVC) have revolutionised our shopping habits as well as our understanding of credit. They are a great boon when used with skill. Unfortunately the day of reckoning always arrives as your card debt has to be paid. The best way to avoid a large debt is to set yourself a limit. If you can't keep to this limit, leave your card at home or cut it up.

One of the major advantages of credit cards is the interest-free period that allows you time to pay for your purchases. This is a great help when you're on a tight budget. Be sure to pay in full and on time. Interest charges on overdue payments can be fierce. The annual fees payable on these cards is more than compensated for by the interest-free time you have to pay. Many cards are linked to commercial operators who offer rewards for points earned in ratio to the amount spent.

There is a sting in this tail. On some cards, if you don't pay the full amount due, interest will be charged, not only on the amount outstanding but on any further purchases you make, these will then be added to the amount on which you are paying interest, then you pay interest on the lot. This can get expensive as outstanding debits on cards attract a high rate of interest.

When your card account arrives each month, take the time to check it thoroughly against your dockets — you don't want to pay for things you didn't purchase. There is only one sensible way to use a credit card — pay in full on the due date.

DEBIT CARDS

Debit cards are linked to your bank account. The amount you spend is debited straight from your account so that instead of borrowing, you are using your own savings — providing they are there! These cards can be used in Automatic Teller Machines (ATMs) and Electronic Fund Transfer at Point of Sale (EFTPOS) which accept credit cards too.

STORE CARDS

Store cards are in the business of making you spend in their store, and some have a point system which offers you free trips, meals and other specials when you use them. The cards are issued free and are relatively easy to obtain from department stores, shopping malls and many big businesses. Be careful of the interest charges. These can blow out as many are substantially higher than the normal credit card charges.

Some stores offer interest-free periods for up to six months, or for special purchase times such as Christmas. These are well worth considering, especially for big items. You are getting goods for nothing for the period of the agreement and, providing you pay on time, the purchase cash for the item can be earning interest for you. There are expensive pitfalls if you don't meet the deadline and pay on time. Again, this scheme is an inducement to buy at this store.

Bits & Bytes

In the late 1890s, the huge US direct marketing company, Sears, Roebuck & Co. gave their loyal mail order customers the first benefits as an inducement to keep shopping. (We never did find out what the benefit was!)

CHARGE CARDS

American Express and Diners Club are two of the best-known charge cards. These differ from credit cards in that there is no period of grace and you must pay all you owe on the due date each month, a good discipline for impulsive spenders. There is an annual fee and they are readily accepted in most countries but not all cards are accepted by every supplier of goods and services.

Always report the loss of a credit or debit card to the issuer as soon as possible in case your card is taken on a spending spree. Never keep your PIN with your card.

STORED VALUE CARDS (SVC)

Stored value cards are the first of the smart cards and they are getting ever smarter in the cashless society that is fast approaching. The first one in general usage was the phonecard. Now nearly every public telephone has been converted to cards rather than cash and vandalism has decreased markedly. The SVCs will remove the weight of small change from our purses and become just another credit card with a fixed value for amounts as low as $5. Some SVCs carry a microchip and can be recharged at your ATM or through an EFTPOS which is linked to your bank account.

Think of the smart card as a small computer, with hardware (a chip) that runs word processing, spreadsheets or graphics. The chip is concerned with money transactions but eventually it may carry personal details like Medicare numbers and who knows what else? This one card could possibly empty your purse of all those other cards that weigh us down, and will help cut card fraud and the forgery of currency.

Smart cards are getting so smart that they can even store foreign currency and keep track of 'loyalty' points, (so you know when you can take that free trip to Europe) and carry your spending money. It can take care of the cost of your entire trip.

Bits & Bytes
The days of the military dogtag hanging around necks are numbered. Armed forces now tend to issue their personnel with smart cards containing all their personal details — a high-tech dogtag!

FINGERSCANNING
The day may be fast approaching when even your PIN number becomes obsolete. A Sydney inventor has developed a biometric system which will enable us to make electronic transactions by simply pressing our finger on a piece of glass no bigger than a postage stamp. Some Australian companies are using it for large fund transfers.

LAY-BY
The lay-by is an ideal way to purchase something you don't need in a hurry and it helps you to keep within your budget. A deposit, usually about 10 per cent, is required, then you sign an agreement and pay off the rest over an agreed interest-free period. There may be a cancellation charge if you change your mind. While you can't walk out with the item straight away, neither do you blow your budget! Lay-bys went out of fashion during the 1980s but they are now making a welcome return.

HIRE PURCHASE
Hire purchase allows you the use of the goods after paying a deposit and agreeing to pay the residue, plus interest, in regular instalments. The goods remain the property of the seller until you have paid them off. You are hiring, paying and using until you own.

RENT AND BUY
Rent and buy plans allow you to rent goods for a fixed time before you buy. While covered by the rental agreement, all repairs are free and you can update the goods although the rental may increase. This is an expensive way to acquire goods, so check it out first.

BALLOON PAYMENT
Balloon payment is another form of hire purchase, often used when buying a car. You agree to a low regular payment with a large final sum. The regular payment 'balloons' at the end.

CREDIT RATING
Everyone has a credit rating. You may not realise it, but somewhere all your credit records are kept in a computer. When you apply for a card or a loan, you grant the creditor access to your file. Any time you apply for a loan it is noted. Most applications are screened by Credit Advantage, which has been keeping files on us all since 1990. It records any defaults on payments, and any applications for credit you may make. This information is protected by the Privacy Act, but the Australian Tax Office, Police Forces and Social Security have easy access to this information.

If you wish to see your ratings file, write to the Credit Advantage office in your state. Mistakes do happen and these files are seldom updated regularly. Even if you have paid off a debt it may not have been recorded, and this could work against you if you apply for another loan.

BANKRUPTCY
Bankruptcy is deep water and, with credit so easy to obtain, more and more people are getting in over their heads. Even just a small loan to buy a fridge can be the one that sends you bankrupt when it comes on top of a mortgage, a car loan and the credit cards.

Another danger occurs when you are running close to the limit of your budget and have not reserved that safety net for the unexpected problems, such as a car accident even one that was not your fault.

If you fail to meet your financial commitment your creditor can sell your assets to meet your debt. If you do not have enough assets you are bankrupt! Once you have been declared a bankrupt, you cannot borrow money, own assets or leave the country until you have discharged the bankruptcy by fulfilling the agreement reached with your creditors.

HOW TO DEAL WITH DEBT

A sensible approach to debt is the way to steer clear of bankruptcy. Firstly, make sure you can service the debt. Sometimes a loan can increase your earning power. For example, if a computer or a car is necessary for your income. Borrow for an asset that will either retain or increase its value. Your home is the prime example but remember that you have to be able to meet the repayments. Try to avoid borrowing for 'wants' rather than 'needs'. For example, if you can't afford the holiday resort go camping!

Be wary if you are asked to serve as guarantor for a family member, friend or partner's debt. It is hard to say 'No' in these circumstances but be aware that as guarantor you are responsible for their debt if they fail to pay back the loan. Be sure you understand the legalese and seek professional advice before you sign anything.

PROBLEMS

Don't panic if you are having financial problems. Look at the situation coldly and calmly. Are you behind on your credit card repayments? If this is the case, your creditors may be willing to negotiate and rearrange your repayments in such a way that you can cope — after all, it is in their interest as well as yours to do so.

You will need to reassess your budget and get your spending under control. List your debts in order of payments due and try to meet the minimum amount due on each one. Pay the ones with the highest interest rates first. Remember, if you can keep your payments going you won't affect your credit rating for the future, when you may want a loan for a house or car.

If the problem is a more serious one, such as suddenly finding yourself unemployed or facing bankruptcy, seek help immediately from your accountant or lawyer. If this doesn't work, help is available from government departments and church groups. Check the front pages of the phonebook. These agencies do not lend money but offer free counselling professional advice on how to set your finances in order.

Bits & Bytes

The rule of 72 is a formula that all bankers and financial whizzes seem to know and use. If you need to know approximately how long it will take for a sum of money you've invested to double, divide 72 by the interest rate at which you've invested. For example, if you have invested $100 at 8 per cent, it will take about nine years to double. This rule works for both credit and debit.

4. BANKING BASICS

• • •

When US bank robber, Willie Sutton, was asked why he robbed banks, he replied:
'Because that's where the money is'.

You've worked out your assets and liabilities, you've got your budget up and running and you are aware of the uses and abuses of credit. Now you're ready to build your wealth and your future and the first thing you need is somewhere, other than under the mattress, to keep your money. A bank is the obvious choice but not the only one. You need access to money so you need an institution offering all financial services: safekeeping of your money, easy withdrawing and depositing with investment and loan facilities. Banks, building societies and credit unions are the traditional keepers of our money, but a growing number of financial companies are joining forces with these providers and forming huge conglomerates that offer a wide variety of services.

All banks, including the new ones, are covered by the *Banking Act* (1959), which requires them to deposit a percentage of their assets in the Reserve Bank of Australia. This is to prevent the kind of 'run' that toppled Wall Street and led to Great Depression of 1929. Under this Act the Reserve Bank can take control of any bank in trouble and the assets deposited with it are made available to restore customers' deposits before other liabilities are repaid.

Building societies were originally formed as non-profit organisations to help with home finance. They have since expanded their services to compete with banks and credit unions. Since Australia deregulated its overseas financial services, building societies have declined. A credit union is a co-operative owned and controlled by the depositors. By depositing money you become a shareholder and are entitled to a vote in the running of the union. Insurance companies, mutual societies and mortgage suppliers are all moving into the world of finance and changing the face of banking.

Bits & Bytes
Our new banknotes are made from polymer, a type of plastic and are equipped with anti-counterfeiting devices, such as microprinted designs incorporated in the polymer and raised print. These polymer notes have a longer life than the old notes.

You may ask: 'How safe is my money?' Nothing is absolutely safe — not even money in a bank — although it is rare for a bank to foreclose. They are kept honest and deposits are protected by the *Banking Act* and, since 1992, the Australian Financial Institutions Commission has regulated building societies and credit unions. Each now has its own independent Banking Ombudsman who is there to resolve any serious complaints you may have about a bank or its staff.

Each bank and institution offers a wide range of accounts and services, but when looked at closely they are all pretty much the same. It is worth noting the difference in their structure. Remember, too, that the rules and charges are constantly changing, as are the managers.

Spending Years Look for the institution that offers what you need as a single person, a partner or a parent. Fees are a killer in these early years and this is the time when you may be more likely to use EFPTOS and ATMs on the spur of the moment without a second thought about charges.

Growth Years The picture has changed and the institution you began with may not be offering the best mortgage rates for your current needs such as an investment property as well as your home, school fees and so on.

Freedom Years Some institutions offer a reduction in fees or fee-free accounts if you are a senior or on a pension. Shop around.

ACCOUNTS: WHAT TO LOOK FOR

Spend time finding the right financial institution and the right type of account. Do you need that chequebook? All those bills we used to pay by cheque (the telephone, the electricity and the insurance) can now be charged to your credit card and you pay them all in one fell swoop. Paying your accounts by phone by debiting your card is cheaper than postage. Another option is to have them paid by 'direct debit', which automatically deducts the payment from your bank account. Even your credit card can be paid this way but charges may be involved. This option makes it essential to keep a close eye on your bank balance to avoid expensive overdraft charges.

Now, of course, you have access to 24-hour banking via your bank's or financial institution's telephone service or on the Internet. All offer a range of services worth looking at, but some cost — do you need them?

A cheque account may be a necessary expense, particularly if you are running your own business, when it becomes a tax deduction. Weigh the pros and cons first.

There are merchant banks and investment houses that offer a chequebook to depositors with a set balance. Others will draw you one of their cheques for a specific amount made out to a particular payee. Your instructions can be phoned in, using an agreed identification or you can give details in writing. We use one of these facilities, based on a cash management account, and it gives us excellent service.

Brochures are an invaluable source of information. Read what the different institutions have to offer in terms of different services: loans, interest rates, cards, accounts, fees. If you can consolidate all your finances into one account, there is only one fee to pay and one account to balance at the end of each month. Each will offer you a different incentive. For example, some will give an exemption from account-keeping fees if a home loan is involved, others may waive fees if you keep your minimum balance above a set amount. There are so many options. Choose the one that suits your needs and remember that as your lifestyle changes so will your banking needs. Keep abreast of what is happening at all times.

Bits & Bytes

On 4 October 1898, the Bank of New South Wales employed its first women, Miss T.B. Miller and Miss E. Lamb, calling them 'lady typewriters'. They were engaged on 12 months probation at the head office in Sydney. Their salary was 80 pounds a year. At the same time the bank purchased its first typewriter and duplicating machine.

IDENTIFICATION

Each time you open a new account with any financial institution, become a signatory to an account or establish a safe custody facility, a government law now requires you to prove your identity. This law is known as the *Financial Transaction Reports Act* 1988 and is designed to assist in the detection of criminal activity and tax evasion.

You will need to complete a few forms and produce various items that establish your identity and add up to the 100 points required by this Act. Such items can include a birth certificate, a passport, a driver's licence, a credit card or your council rate notice. If you are under 18 years you need to provide only one form of identification. Special provisions also apply to Aborigines from remote areas, recent arrivals in the country, non-residents and some recipients of social security benefits.

The institution will also ask you to provide personal information, such as your occupation, employer and any other relevant financial details. It is obliged to keep any information about you confidential, unless the law requires it to reveal details to the

Australian Taxation Office or other authorities — you will be advised if this is the case. If you believe that information about you has been deliberately misused, call the Privacy Hotline in your state.

Bits & Bytes
The Bank of New South Wales employed its third woman in 1907, again in the Sydney office. The first woman appointed outside Sydney was Miss E.B. Pocock, who joined the Brisbane office in 1911. It was not until World War I that the general employment of women came about. By the end of the war 279 women were employed Australia-wide.

TAX FILE NUMBER
Under the *Taxation Laws Amendment (Tax File Numbers) Act* 1988, all financial institutions are required to deduct tax at the highest marginal rate, including the Medicare levy, from any interest, dividend or distribution you receive, unless you provide your tax file number. It is not compulsory to provide your tax file number. However, if you don't provide it, the highest rate of tax will be deducted from your income and you will have to wait until the next tax year to claim it as a credit for tax prepaid — less money to spend or save that year!

Anyone who has lodged a tax return automatically has a tax file number. If you haven't received one or have forgotten it, apply to your local branch of the tax office. Anyone under 16 years earning less than $420 p.a., most age pensioners, and religious and voluntary organisations need not supply their tax file number. These people need simply complete a form, available at the bank. Remember to call the Privacy Hotline if you think your tax file number has been misused.

ELECTRONIC BANKING

ATM (Automatic Teller Machine), EFTPOS (Electronic Fund Transfer at Point of Sale), phone banking and the Internet are all part of the new (and sometimes worrying) world of banking. These facilities are here to stay and the banks are encouraging us to use them as they close more and more branches. The key to using this electronic world is your PIN. It is your financial lifeline.

Your PIN (Personal Identification Number) is your signature. It is part of today's electronic world and you will need it, not just to access money but as entry into mobile phone systems and security doors as well as many things to come.

Most institutions let you choose your own, so you are more likely to remember it. Your PIN number is personal, private and precious so memorise it and never write it down. Anyone with access to your PIN can strip you of your savings and put you into debt. Protect it.

ATMs and EFTPOS make banking life easy. Your card and PIN come into their own as they give you the extra flexibility of interlinking networks, allowing you to use most ATMs and EFTPOS and to do your banking out of business hours anywhere in the country. Fees are charged for the use of EFTPOS and other institutions' ATMs. Watch for these unnecessary costs, think before you withdraw: it costs as much to withdraw $19 as it does to withdraw $99! Take care when withdrawing from ATMs, it is very easy to be seen collecting a handful of notes.

Phone and Internet banking is now offered by most institutions. It is simple and easy to use. It gives you 24-hour access to your account to check on your balance and deposit details, transfers to other accounts, order a statement, or use BPAY® to pay accounts.

Electronic banking removes the need to carry lots of cash, which is particularly handy when travelling.

Home ATMs may be here in the not too distant future. (Of course, $100 notes will not appear like magic in your kitchen.) A home ATM would enable you to transfer cash value to the computer chip of a stored value or 'smart card' and transfer credits and debits between accounts, pay bills and check your balance.

DEPOSITS AND WITHDRAWALS

Deposits can be made over the counter or through an ATM. Salaries, pensions, interest or dividends can be paid directly into your account. This method saves you waiting for the mail, or going to the bank to make a deposit into your account. It is there on the due date, earning interest, and you can use it immediately.

Your bills can be paid in various ways. You can pay by cheque but remember that you have a limited number of fee-free transactions a month. EFTPOS also costs but gives you the convenience of shopping and, at the same time, getting cash out of banking hours. You can have regular payments made as an automatic debit or you can pay accounts by your credit card — each counting as one transaction in that month. If you use cash, remember to keep a record of the transaction as proof of payment, or (for your tax return) if the expenditure is related to the earning of income.

A cheque is a written instruction to your institution to pay a sum of money on demand. It is convenient, safe and easy to carry and there are simple rules for their use. Always make certain you have enough cleared funds available to meet the cheque. Fill in the empty spaces on the 'pay' and 'the sum of' lines with a horizontal line and never use a pencil or sign a blank cheque. Crossing a cheque with two parallel lines tells the bank not to cash it across the counter — it must be paid into a bank account. The cheque butt is your record of the transaction and is essential to reconciling the statement of your account.

> **Peggy** When I was In Italy a few years ago I purchased a gold goat from a jeweller on the Rialto in Venice, as a retirement present to myself. The shop accepted my personal Australian bank cheque and quoted me in Australian dollars. I wrote the amount quoted on the cheque in the normal way. When my bank statement came some months later I found it had been paid in US dollars, adding considerably to the cost. The moral of this story is always write 'Australian Dollars' when

cashing a cheque overseas. Safer still, put it on a credit card.

STATEMENTS

We recommend monthly rather than quarterly statements because it is easier to pick up your mistakes each month rather than having to plough back through transactions over several months. Your balance can vary according to bank charges.

Statements show all transactions: deposits, withdrawals, interest paid or received, automatic payments and deposits, and fees. When you receive your statement, tick off all payments and deposits on the statement and match them against your records. You can easily see any missing payments or deposits and adjust your records to the statement until you and the bank balance.

Passbook accounts seldom generate statements as the transactions are recorded in the book. The only way to keep records of what the deposits and withdrawals cover is to keep a record in a separate book, noting what you have put in and taken out, or write a note beside each entry in the passbook.

Look for bank charges on your statement, see how much they are costing and cut down on transactions, particularly other banks' ATMs and EFTPOS.

For all types of accounts the easiest way to record all money movements is to keep a cashbook. All you need is a cheap cashbook with as many columns as you have expenses. Keep a separate page for your income and another for your expenditure. Adjust this example to your needs for each financial account:

Cashbook — Income

Date	Source	Bank	Amount	Salary	Interest	Dividend	Transfer	Sundries

Cashbook — Expenditure

Date	Chq/No.	Amount	Charges	Mortgage	Living	Entertain	Phone/etc	Sundries

THE COSTS OF BANKING

Banks and other institutions are in the business of making money — everything costs. The information they give out is bewildering and complex. The only advice we can give is to allocate a day or so to reading and listing the various charges. Then adjust your banking habits to take advantage of the most economical account that suits your needs.

Charges are changing all the time so keep up-to-date. You will get a fair idea of these by watching your bank statement. Loyalty to your bank, or from your bank, is a thing of the past. If you are not tied by a loan or mortgage, change banks if the opposition looks better.

If you move money between your accounts, even at the same institution, you may be hit with some charges, so ask before you transfer.

REDUCING FEES

By keeping track of bank charges and adjusting your banking habits to any changes to transaction costs, you can reduce considerably the debits to your account. Beware of accounts that require you to keep a hefty minimum credit balance, some up to $2,000, to receive a fee exemption or a fee reduction on your cheques or transactions. The interest paid on these accounts is minimal. A rethink of your bill paying habits could see you investing that $2,000 in a high interest bearing deposit. Make sure you are not given an account linked to cheque facilities that you may not want as the conditions the bank imposes can be tougher.

The bottom line is that the small customer's bank account is uneconomical and we can expect to be hit continually as the banks try to protect their profits or make more. Explore every avenue to keep fees under control.

If you monitor your banking habits and your bank regularly, you'll bank the benefits.

If something is unclear or doesn't make sense, ask for an explanation. Keep all transaction documentation.

The traditional role of the bank is fast disappearing, along with local branches. One-stop money shops are here to stay and you can now deposit, withdraw, check on accountant balances, pay credit cards, and many other accounts, at post offices, supermarkets and shopping centres.

It is all very simple at these new outlets — you swipe a card through a reader, key in your PIN and away you go. Soon we may not need a bank at all, nor will we worry if loans, deposits, management of our superannuation or advice on our finances is provided by an insurance company or by a range of companies accessed through a home computer on the Internet.

Internet banking is quick and convenient, no more waiting in queues. All you need is your personal computer connected to the Internet and it will cost you only a local call to check your accounts, move your money around, pay accounts including loans, get the latest interest rates and financial news — all without leaving your desk.

Bits and Bytes
The world's dimmest bank robber has to be
Homer Lawyer, who wrote his name and address
on the back of the hold-up note!

5. ON YOUR WAY

• • •

> There are two times in life when you should not speculate:
> when you can't afford it, and when you can.
> *Mark Twain*

Women were once ignored by most of the 'high rollers' in the financial world. In the early 1980s it was impossible for a single woman to get a home loan. Now that more of us are earning our own money, the experts are falling over themselves to tell us what we should be doing with it. Information never goes amiss so, sift it and make your own informed decision.

Even $100 is enough for your first venture into making your money grow through investments. In fact, an astute collector can turn a $5 phonecard into a growing investment. Investment is about creating income to secure your home, educate the children, have money for luxuries and protect your future. The most common way to predict the future movement of wealth is to examine past records. In the financial arena (though it never repeats itself exactly) a pattern does emerge over time and the experts call it the 'historical element'. In 1937 the London newspaper, *The Evening Standard*, published an 'Investment Clock', which has been used as a guide to market cycles ever since.

THE INVESTMENT CLOCK

Time has shown that this clock is fairly accurate and that the cycles tend to run between eight and eleven years. If you understand this, you won't rush out to buy a product when it is 'fashionable' and then sell it the moment there is a hiccup in the market. This

The Investment Clock

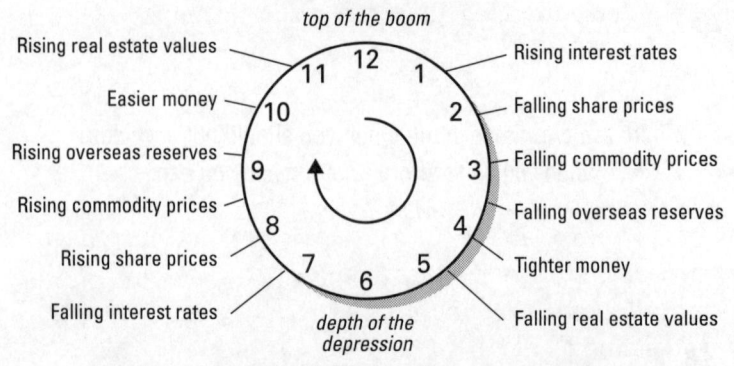

top of the boom

- 12/1:
- Rising real estate values (11)
- Easier money (10)
- Rising overseas reserves (9)
- Rising commodity prices (8)
- Rising share prices (7)
- Falling interest rates

depth of the depression (6)

- Rising interest rates (1)
- Falling share prices (2)
- Falling commodity prices (3)
- Falling overseas reserves (4)
- Tighter money (5)
- Falling real estate values

Note: Share prices first to fall in a downturn; first to recover in an upturn. Real estate last to fall, last to recover

knowledge will give you a much better chance of making your investments grow.

It is interesting to look at the past 100 years. In that time there have been downturns (depressions) in the market during 1897, 1907, 1921, 1932, 1937, 1949, 1961, 1974, 1982 and 1990. In the long run the graph has always continued to rise, in spite of these hiccups.

We have tried to stick to core investments and as we have 'balanced' our portfolio, we have so far survived these bumps unscathed.

Security is the first thing that springs to mind when it comes to making hard-earned money grow but nothing can be guaranteed as being totally secure. Making sensible investments and understanding the money market will reduce the security risk and, if handled properly, you will see your money grow.

If you have only a small amount to invest and can't afford to replace it if it is lost, don't rush out and put your money into high-risk shares. Look at products offered by financial institutions, especially those with a capital guarantee clause. Remember to check if there is an expiry date for that guarantee — ask questions and read all the fine print.

To begin your investment plan, decide what you are trying to achieve: income or capital growth or a combination of both. Your stage of life and its current needs as well as your future needs and wants will influence this decision. No single strategy suits everyone, investments have to be planned. Seek expert advice before you start.

> **Judi** I work in the world of finance so my husband has always left the managing and planning of the family's money to me. Now that the children have fled the nest and set up alone, there is more cash flow available so we are looking to secure our own future. After a lot of research I have decided to build an investment property portfolio as our retirement fund, over and above our super. This seems the ideal way for us to go as I plan to gain a steady income from the properties, we will be able to enjoy spending while keeping our capital expenditure intact. What has been interesting was my parents' reaction when they heard of my role as the 'money manager'. Neither of them really approve, they can't understand why my husband allows it!

Spending years Think capital growth. You have time on your side to make tremendous gains with shares, property or collectables. You could also take the odd risk for a higher return, or even try your forecasting skills in the futures market, though this area requires expert knowledge. Plan for the dreams you have for the growth years. Some medium term investments are a good idea for this — consider 10-year bonds as well.

Growth years Consolidate, rationalise and add to your portfolio. This is the time when you can reap the benefits from early investments and indulge in a sports car or holiday house. Remember that the older the children get, the more expensive they become. Invest spare cash for a quick, safe return from bank bills or short-term deposits with that floating capital.

Freedom years Look for the best results for a steady income, as capital growth is not so important now. Invest the essential amount in a long-term safe place, to give you the security and income you need — it won't earn anything under the bed! Blue chip shares are sound but now is probably a good time to stop any dividend reinvestment plans you have elected to take on. It is better to enjoy the cash from dividends rather than the increase in capital and all that bookkeeping.

INVESTMENT PLANNING

Women are still not retiring with the same benefits that their male counterparts have gained. Investment planning simply means identifying what you want, when you want it and the best way to get it. Examine the advantages and disadvantages of the investments in the context of your specific stage of money management. The younger you are the longer you have to achieve a particular financial goal.

'Don't put all your eggs in one basket' or 'spread your risk' are the most common pieces of advice you will hear from friends, family and advisers. It's not bad advice, but remember that there is a trade-off between high risk with high return and slow but steady growth with a lower return. When considering a high return, the bottom line is what you can afford. Wise investors balance their portfolio between risk, growth and safety. Be comfortable with your investment to avoid sleepless nights. Start with your $100 and add to it regularly.

To achieve a balance, we spread our money over a wide range of investments: cash split between term deposit and cash management; mostly blue chip shares (at our age we do not need many risks) and residential apartments, limited to two bedrooms (fewer sub-tenants), in good rental areas. We prefer to have an agent manage our real estate leaving us free to travel but when it comes to the management of cash and shares, we do our own — email is our answer here.

Investment decisions can be covered in five broad categories: strategy, income, growth, accumulation, and protection. At each stage of your life the importance of these five categories will change and affect the investment choices you make. It is important to realise this and not allow yourself to become set in your ways of handling your money. Always remember that money is a volatile animal.

Strategy This is the overall investment plan which takes into consideration your needs and objectives. If you require a regular income from your investments, then it must be part of the strategy. You should make sure that the money will be accessible, without hefty charges or capital losses, in case an emergency or major expense suddenly arises.

Income Earning a regular cash flow is important at every age, and a well planned investment portfolio will supply an income when you need it. This is particularly important once you reach the freedom years. The type of investment you select should always take into account that an emergency can arise at any time, so check how long it will take to get your money out and what it would cost.

Growth Vital in every financial plan. Shares, investment properties and some trusts offer growth over inflation in the long term, so the earlier you start these the bigger your capital growth. Short-term growth, which we all need at some stage, can be achieved through cash management trusts and term deposits.

Bits & Bytes
If you are offered an investment with the promise of an unusually high rate of return, it is probably a very risky deal. The risk level must always be acceptable to you.

Accumulation This can happen only if you are disciplined with your budget and your saving, making sure both are working at the highest possible rates. Inflation must be taken into consideration with all your investment strategies. It will reduce the buying power of money over time, so your investments must increase at a rate higher than the inflation rate to keep you ahead.

Protection This is essential at all stages of your life. Insurance in all its forms — savings, health, home, car and income protection — is a safety net that provides some peace of mind. It is needed at all ages, just like a will.

INVESTMENT — A RISK?
Our answer is *no*! Everything is a risk, depending on your state of mind. The degree of an investment risk depends on your understanding of what you are planning and doing with your money. You can take a 'punt' where you could lose the lot or make a fortune — either way you learn! Punting is risky, so let common sense rule the day.

The guidelines we suggest for 'safe' investment are diversification, quality, tax, expectations and expert advice.

Diversification Spread your money over a variety of investments. A portfolio that is well balanced with shares, fixed term interest, real estate and trusts has spread the risk. One section of your portfolio may slide, another may rise and in the long run, diversification evens things out. This will be obvious when the share market has a hiccup and interest rates are more likely to move.

Quality Quality is a better option than quantity in any investment plan. By choosing to buy blue chip shares that pay reasonable dividends you are more likely to gain a safe yearly income, with tax advantages and a potential for capital growth. Carefully chosen real estate has much the same advantages.

Tax We all pay it and we all want to minimise it. If you have retired or are living on your investments you are a 'captive' taxpayer with very few opportunities to acquire tax breaks. Fully franked dividends from shares are one option, negative gearing on shares and property is another. Most importantly, you can go broke by trying to reduce tax, so ask for advice.

Expectations Good past results do not guarantee good future results so consider them a guide. Research is the key, whether you are looking at trusts, shares, real estate or the money market.

Expert advice Along this investment road you are going to need advice and help. There are hundreds of books on the subject of how to invest, including this one. Look at the index, if it covers what you want, read it and take notes as you go. We recommend you gain a basic knowledge of the subject before you seek advice from the 'experts' otherwise the jargon will bamboozle.

ADVICE: WHERE TO GO
Financial advisers/planners

These are the experts we need when we do not have the desire, the time or the knowledge to develop our own investment strategy. Choosing the right adviser for your particular needs and plans is a big decision, and research and some knowledge of the language is essential. Find an adviser you feel you will have confidence in. Check their credentials, expertise and fees. Free advice is always available at your bank though it may be loaded in their favour.

Under the Corporations Law it is an offence for a person to give financial advice unless they are licensed (or an authorised representative of a licence holder) by the Australian Securities and Investments Commission (ASIC). Advisers should also be members of the Financial Planning Association of Australia (FPA). Both of these organisations and the Australian Stock Exchange (ASX) have lists of licensed advisers available: just phone them or visit their website.

It is essential to know how your adviser is paid. Some receive a commission on your investment, some have a scale of fees based on the amount you invest, others receive a combination of both. You need to ask if there is an association with any of the providers they recommend. For example, many advisers are associated with an insurance company, a financial institution or one of the banks, which means you may not receive truly impartial advice.

One of the questions to ask advisers and planners is whether they include an ongoing monitoring service of your portfolio in the quoted fee. Finally, check that they carry professional indemnity insurance. If in doubt about anything, seek a second opinion.

Financial advisers and planners are trying to sell you their ideas and plans. The final choice must be yours. Be sure you fully understand the required State of Advice (SOA) which is their written statement setting out their advice. You must understand all the implications and feel that the plan meets your needs. Take the time to read it thoroughly, do not be rushed into signing then and there. Remember that you are their bread and butter.

Margaret The sudden death of my husband, who was one of the traditional ones, left me floundering, especially when I had to cope with his business. He was a sole trader and I knew I had to sell it as quickly as possible. Coping with this and the money from the sale almost overwhelmed me. I had no idea of what to do with it and I had no desire to manage it myself. For a short time I thought I would give most of it to the children. In fact, I was frightened and left it sitting in a bank account. Finally I consulted several financial advisers and ended up confused and bewildered, each one having advised entirely different schemes. Now I have taken the time to read and research and have formulated a portfolio of short-term capital growth with a regular income component — blue chip shares, term deposits. I am even thinking of buying a property when the right opportunity offers.

Stockbrockers

Stockbrokers are the traders in shares on the Australian Stock Exchange (ASX). While other investment advisers may give advice, ultimately you need a broker to invest on the market. One of the major functions of a broker is to buy and sell as instructed by the investor. They may also give responsible advice on starting and running a portfolio of shares, debentures, futures, trusts, commodities, in fact, anything trading on the money market. To become a stockbroker they have to be of good character with proven business integrity and appropriate tertiary qualifications. They must pay a large joining fee to become a member of the ASX.

The ASX offers a stockbroker referral service which will put you in touch with a broker. Stockbrokers generally do not charge for their advice, but they do charge a brokerage fee for buying and selling based on a percentage of the sum involved. This full service brokerage fee is high to cover the broker's knowledge and research which they are passing on to you.

When you become an established client, your broker may send you reports on any new investment he feels would enhance your portfolio. They provide regular reports on the market in general, including advice on 'buy, hold or sell' opportunities. Every three to six months you may receive a spreadsheet listing your investments value of the day. This enables you to keep control and make any adjustments necessary.

Most brokers will negotiate a discount on fees, so remember to ask about this when you become a regular trader. Some 'discount' brokers trade at a reduced rate, but give no advice on what to buy or sell. Nor do they give you a periodic report on the market and your holding. It is a limited service but, once you know what you are doing and fully understand the market, discount brokers are worth considering. For all Internet trading you must know exactly what you are doing. It is instant which means you could win or lose 'your millions' in that instant.

The National Guarantee Fund (NGF), constituted under and governed by the Corporations Law, protects investors from unscrupulous operators. If your broker has run off with your money (most unlikely), this fund will act for you. The ASX will advise you on this.

Fund Managers

These are the investment company people who manage your money as a team when you invest in a unit trust or other managed investment products, even superannuation. They are responsible for running the fund and deciding when and where to invest. It is necessary to ask a few questions before handing over your money to their care. Ask how long that particular investment has been in existence, and the return so far. Take home the brochures and, if you feel comfortable, then that's the one to go with. If not, keep looking and asking questions. It is their knowledge of the markets and how they handle the rises and falls that you need to trust. You will receive regular reports, statements of your investments and details for your tax returns.

Legal practitioners

Lawyers (solicitors) may have a knowledge of and access to the financial world. Many have private clients who will lend money to other clients who pay interest to the lender. An agreement is drawn up between the borrower and the lender. Lawyers must pass the required professional courses and are strictly regulated by governments and the Law Society. They pay into a large indemnity and fidelity fund. Building a good relationship with your lawyer is an asset. Seek his/her advice if you are in doubt about any move you are contemplating.

Accountants

Accountants will give you financial advice — after all, they are licensed experts at balancing the books. As your portfolio grows, your bookkeeping and your tax return will become very time-consuming and complicated. You should look for an accountant you can communicate with and who understands your requirements. All are bound by the rules of their associations and most can invest your money in most financial areas, apart from the stock market.

The Australian Securities and Investments Commission does not require accountants to hold a licence. They accept that their training and experience gives them the required skills to be advisers but they must belong to their professional body.

Bankers

Bankers are in the ideal situation to know the money world. There are financial advisers in most banks and this is becoming a larger part of banks' business. The advice is usually free but inclined to lean towards their own bank's services. They are not into speculation and offer a safe route to investment. They will run your portfolio or start you off.

Real estate agents and valuers

These experts play an important part in the property market. Their association has laid down a code of conduct and rules and the main overseeing body in each state is the consumer protection agency. To be registered, they must pass a licensing course approved by a government authority.

Traders in collectables

Traders and auctioneers of collectables have their own professional association and rules for each special area. If the image of Steptoe & Son haunts you, deal only with one of their members. The corporate world has invested many millions in art, antiques and collectables. It has become a large and important part of the financial world, but be cautious.

Friends and relatives

They might be a mine of information and help, but make sure you dig deep in the mine and sift it well! Often family and friends think they know best and sometimes do. All 'hot tips' should be looked at with cautious eyes.

All these skilled financial advisers are there to help you make your first step into the investment world and you may decide to stay with one throughout your investment life. You may prefer to do-it-yourself and experience the thrill of judging the market. Whatever way you go, you must also keep in mind the invisible factor of the financial world — inflation, up or down, must influence all areas.

If you have to water it or feed it — think twice before investing your money in it.

THE TOOLS OF INVESTMENT
Interest

Interest has many meanings: it can mean curiosity, stimulation, advantage, or a right to a share in property or business. It is also a charge for the use of borrowed money and this is the meaning we are concerned with here.

The basis of all simple investments is interest. It is the percentage return you receive for making your money work or lending it. This covers many forms of investment, but essentially the borrower pays interest for the use of money at a rate and length of time agreed to by both parties before the contract is written. Understanding simple and compound interest rates is necessary for making choices and comparing the many investment options that will confront you.

Investing at a simple (or nominal) rate of interest means income with no capital growth. At the end of the agreed term your money will have earned only the agreed percentage. If you choose to re-invest your interest (which will mean you earn interest on interest) you have growth but no direct income — this is compound interest.

If the interest is compounded quarterly, monthly or even more frequently, the benefits are considerable and your capital grows like magic.

For example, suppose you invest $10,000 at 10 per cent over three years: simple and compound will give these results:

	Simple		Compound	
	Principal	*Interest*	*Principal*	*Interest*
First year	10,000	1,000	10,000	1,000
Second year	10,000	1,000	11,000	1,100
Third year	10,000	1,000	12,100	1,210
Total interest		**3,000**		**3,310**

Source: Nicholas Ingram

The other side of interest is when you borrow. In this case, pay back what you have borrowed plus interest. Hopefully, what you have purchased with the borrowed money will grow in value. There are many variations of a mortgage agreement on property. Look at them all carefully and assess the advantages and disadvantages of each.

A drop in the official interest rate is great news for borrowers, especially those with a home loan. For those who live on investment income, particularly self-funded retirees, a drop in interest rates is not pleasant, as the costs of goods and services may rise but income will fall.

Dollar cost averaging

This is a method of investing that has proved to be of value over good times and bad times. It is mainly used for market-linked investments. You invest a set amount regularly, no matter what the market is doing. If it rises, your money will purchase fewer units but the units you already hold will increase in value. If it falls, your money buys more units but conversely your unit value will fall. You need to stick at it over a lengthy period to make it work, the theory being that you should come out in front over a period. It is also a disciplined way of saving.

You can make this work for yourself. You could decide to buy $500 worth of shares on a specific day every three or six months. This is a long-term bet and if you are young it really can work for you over time.

Gearing

Gearing simply means borrowing money to invest. This is also known as investment leverage. Borrowing always incurs cost: that is, interest. Negative gearing occurs when the interest payable is more than the income. You then use the excess debt over income, or the loss, as a tax deduction on other income. It can be an advantage with any form of investment providing it is a future income-earning project or has prospects of capital gains and you can afford to service the loan.

Borrowing money to buy an investment property is the most common use of negative gearing. When the income from the rent is not enough to cover the interest on the loan, you are subsidising this debt from other income. This negative gearing reduces your taxable income and, hopefully, produces capital gain over time. Leverage usually needs at least five years to work. Gearing into shares can be even more tax effective as shares often carry franked dividends, which further reduce your overall tax. This means borrowing for an investment in which you are looking for long-term capital gain, and is an area where advice is essential.

Don't negative gear unless you are sure you can service the loan.

Superannuation

Superannuation is very much in everyone's mind. The government's compulsory superannuation has been implemented to make us more responsible for our own retirement. As the post-war baby boomers reach pension age, even the expanded Superannuation Guarantee (whereby both employers and employees pay in more and more) will not enable us to retire in the manner we dream about. We will need additional income.

Super is a very tax-effective investment and it is a good 'no touch' way to add to your retirement nest egg. It is worth continually adding to your contribution. Again, seek an expert on super for advice to avoid extending yourself too much.

Inflation

The 'thief' that steals your money and erodes your investment. The purchasing power of $100 in 1970 was reduced to $15.70 by 1994, so your capital must be assessed in real terms (purchasing power), not in nominal terms (face value). This makes it essential to have a sound investment strategy that takes inflation into account. Ignore its effects at your peril. Your money should be earning an after-tax rate of return that is greater than inflation.

One measure of inflation is the Consumer Price Index (CPI), which is announced each quarter. CPI changes are based on a set 'basket' of consumer goods and services which is used to assess the rise or fall of the cost of living over each period. The Reserve Bank does its best to control inflation by raising and lowering official interest rates. It does not always succeed, as we found in the 1980s. Worldwide central banks spend lots of time trying to get the balance right.

Growth investments over the long term, such as shares and property are considered by many to be the best way to combat the effects of inflation.

Bits & Bytes
During the American War of Independence (1775-1778) inflation was so bad that the price of wheat rose by 14,000 per cent and the price of beef by 33,000 per cent.

6. INVESTMENT OPTIONS

● ● ●

Caveat Emptor: let the buyer beware.
Take responsibility for your own decisions.

Investment is a personal matter and it is as varied as the people involved. It is up to you to decide on the mix of investments you will make to achieve your financial freedom and goals. In the end it comes down to three basics which you combine and use to suit your aims — security, income and capital gain.

We have already recommended a diversified investment portfolio as the basis for sound investing, taking into account both your current and future needs and wants. By spreading your assets across a range of different investments the theory is (and we have proved it) that you reduce the risk element while receiving an acceptable return, plus a capital growth.

The share market crash of 1987 is a good example of the danger of not diversifying your investments. Anyone who had all their savings invested in shares would have been in a tough position if they had needed cash in a hurry. Equally, for those who could afford to ride out this temporary downturn, the share market rose well above that 1987 value within a few years.

Investment is not something you do once then leave alone to look after itself. It must be monitored regularly to keep up with your changing lifestyle. The choices you make will depend on what stage you have reached in your life and what you have planned for the future. It all comes down to your short, medium and long-term goals for each stage of your money management.

Spending years During these years you are likely to think of the short term only — understandable but not practical. Certainly have investments for your short-term needs and wants, but don't forget the medium and long term. As we keep saying, this is the one time in your life when you can really secure your future with sound investments.

Growth years By now you will have controlled the short-term spending sprees but you will still need short-term investments to cover any worn out labour-saving items in the home or spiralling education expenses. The medium and long-term investments you have in place will need to be reassessed and updated.

Freedom years You will be watching your investments carefully and moving long-term investments to short-term areas for ease of access, as you find your needs now demand. Don't rest on your laurels — keep your money working. If you think of your retirement as a 25-year plus holiday you will appreciate why your investments still have to work!

GOALS: SHORT, MEDIUM & LONG-TERM

Short term means up to three years. You need to look at putting your money in an investment that will give you the best possible return, yet allows you ease of access without monetary penalties. For example, look at cash management trusts, or a savings account. The choice you make is based on the interest offered, its frequency of payment and your specific goal.

Medium term is anything from four to nine years. Medium-term goals involve accumulating money for those larger items in life and should be chosen with growth in mind. The investments to consider here are shares, debentures, fixed interest investments and trusts. The choice will depend on what market forces are prevailing at the time when you have money to invest. If shares are at the top of their range you would be wise to look at debentures or even a long-term deposit. It's all back to keeping your finger on the pulse, being market-wise and doing that research.

Long term is exactly that, saving for well down the track — at least ten years. This is your retirement fund you will need in addition to any super or pension you expect to receive. Superannuation is one of the best options for long-term investment but not the only one. Look also at shares, investment properties, trusts and bonds. Go for growth and choose investments that will generate an income through regular returns as well as providing some tax relief.

The comparison of returns between all investments is an essential mathematical nightmare! To know where to invest to suit your particular needs, you'll need an indication of the net income each type of investment brings in to enable you to make an informed decision.

Bits & Bytes
It is just as important to diversify within an investment as it is to diversify between investments.

INVESTMENT OPTIONS
Investment options come in various forms. The main ones are:
- Interest-bearing deposits
- Unit trusts
- Collectables
- Shares
- Real estate

Interest-bearing deposits
These provide an easy way to make your money work. They offer no tax credits or capital increase — the interest percentage return is all you get. They are available from banks, building societies, credit unions and many other financial institutions, and include

term deposits, cash management trusts, debentures, government and semi-government bonds and bank bills.

Cash investments, either in fixed term or floating, have no component for capital growth. The capital that comes out at the end of the term is the same amount you put in. It bears interest during its term and that is it. The advantage is security. Fixed terms tend to be very secure for your funds and you know exactly what your return will be. There are no tax advantages — you will be fully taxed on your interest income and the tax is charged in the same financial year as it is received. You are, again, a 'captive' taxpayer.

This form of investment is an ideal place to park spare cash while you research and save for longer term and capital growth investments. It helps you plan your cash flow and gives you the flexibility to organise the frequency of interest payments to meet expenses. In a well-balanced portfolio you need this kind of safe cash backstop.

Term deposits involve giving the use of your money for an agreed term at an agreed interest rate. There are no entry, exit or management fees. They are ideal for small investors, with most institutions taking as little as $500-$1,000. As a added bonus, if you don't need the interest income to supplement your everyday living, you can usually arrange for the capital, with the interest added, to be reinvested at the end of the term. By doing this you are increasing your rate of saving and the capital invested.

There are a few slight disadvantages. If the returns on other investments take a big jump upwards, you miss out, you are tied to the agreed rate for the agreed term. If you suddenly have a cash flow problem the institution is not obliged to release your money early, and if they do agree, there may be a hefty fee. Of course, there is no capital growth unless you invest your interest in the next term.

The rates of interest and frequency of payment will vary from one institution to the next and so do the nominated terms of your investment: either 'short' (under 12 months) or 'long' (2–5 or

10 years). When the investment matures don't rush to reinvest in the same institution. Although it is the easy way out when we have other pressures on our time. Make the time to research other options.

Cash management trusts They give you the freedom to put in and take out at any time. CMTs pool your money with that of other investors to play the short-term money market. The interest rates are usually calculated on your daily balance and vary according to the rate of the day. Returns are usually paid quarterly. A CMT works well as a short-term investment as it offers a higher interest rate than banks. Most CMTs offer telephone withdrawal and some have chequebook facilities — handy but may invoke fees.

CMTs have minimum requirements for both deposits and withdrawals and they do not deal in cash. The initial opening deposit is quite large and your interest rate can be lowered if your account drops below the set limit. Again, they offer no capital growth, but you can add to your capital by reinvesting your interest — compound interest.

Debentures These are loans made to a company at a fixed rate of interest for a fixed term. They are a readily negotiable investment as they can be bought and sold. The loan is secured by a first charge over the company's tangible assets which makes them one of the safer forms of investment. Mortgage debentures are issued over land owned by the company, secured by a registered first mortgage.

Unsecured notes These are issued by companies to raise money for a fixed period and interest, and are unsecured by any company assets. They therefore rank well down in the pecking order in the event of a wind-up. To compensate for this risk, the interest rate is higher than on secured notes.

Government and semi-government bonds Also known as coupon payments, these are a guaranteed loan to these bodies for a fixed period and at fixed interest. They can be purchased at the beginning of their life from the issuing body. They are traded on the open market at any time during their term, but the number of coupons used and the movement of interest rates will influence the price. The return is paid twice a year and their price on the exchange will rise as that day approaches. If general interest rates rise, the market price of bonds will fall as the money market will give a better rate and, vice versa: if general interest rates fall the bond coupon will give a better return and therefore the bond price rises.

These bonds certainly have a potential for capital gains or losses. If you buy a $100 bond with interest set at 10 per cent, each coupon is worth $10 p.a. If the general interest rate falls from 10 per cent to 9 per cent, the market will perceive the bond to be worth $110, a better return than what the current market is offering. You sell your bond, make $10 capital gain and you still have the original $100 in hand to invest again. For those mathematically inclined, $10 divided by $110 equals 9 per cent.

> Interest rates fall = bond prices rise
> Interest rates rise = bond prices fall

Bonds are a very safe long-term investment and they are negotiable, a definite advantage for women during those 'climbing' years.

Bank Bills are bills of exchange drawn by one bank on another. They are issued for 30, 60, 90 or 180 days and have a set rate of interest. These are a good place to 'rest' spare cash and are available through a bank.

Unit trusts: Funds under management
Unit trusts are a type of managed fund offering a wide range of investments, which makes them particularly interesting and advantageous to women who are starting out on the money trail with as little as $1,000 to invest. Unit trusts are formed to invest in

property and mortgage; local and international shares; cash and fixed interest, or a mixture of investments. There must be an approved Trust Deed lodged with the Australian Securities and Investment Commission and a registered prospectus which gives the details and responsibilities of the trustees, the fund managers and the objectives of the trust.

Each unit trust is made up of units of equal value and the number you have depends on the amount you invest. The price of units can move up or down according to how the value of the trust's assets moves. There are fees to be paid, usually on entrance as well as an annual management fee and an exit fee. Understand these costs before you hand over any of your hard-saved cash. The profits of the unit trust are distributed as dividends but the first call on profits is to pay the fund managers — no one works for nothing!

> Market up = unit price up
> Market down = unit price down

Unit trusts are a good starting-point for your portfolio. The initial deposit is usually a set amount. However, once you are an established unit holder most trusts will accept as little as $100 as an addition to your holding. The risk and the potential to earn are spread over all unit trust members. Managers handle the business of managing, reporting, buying and selling, taking the hassle out of investing. There can be tax advantages and at the end of the financial year you will receive a full statement of earning, tax credits (if any) and depreciation, making your tax return much easier to complete.

Trust units can be converted to cash if needed but allow at least five working days. Plan your exit ahead, watch the market and the interest payment dates. If the interest payment has just been made the unit price may be lower, and include the exit fees in your calculations. Your broker, accountant, investment adviser, banker or solicitor can advise you and invest for you in this area. You can also buy direct from the trust itself.

A wide range of trusts and managed funds are available from insurance companies, banks and investment firms. Income can be paid at any interval, from monthly to yearly. Earnings can be paid by cheque or directly into your bank by electronic transfer.

Listed equity or share funds are pooled funds acquired from all types of investors, small or large. You buy units in a trust at the price set by the market value of the shares held by the trust. As the share values rise and fall so does the value of the units. If any overseas shares are held by the trust, the exchange rate for the relevant currency influences the price. They are a practical way to enter the share market, especially when you don't have thousands to spare. They also take the hassle out of managing your own portfolio. You don't have to keep involved records and you still have the fun of watching and playing the market.

You can diversify with just a small outlay. There are trusts that offer investment in all sections of the Australian and overseas markets. Others specialise in a particular area — ecological, blue chip only, second level companies or minerals and mining trusts, the choice is wide.

The fund manager will follow the market, buying and selling as indicated on the day, so your return is averaged over a period of time. By spreading your money over a large number of shares this is a low risk investment. If one company fails, there are others that will succeed. The selection of shares bought and sold by the fund is the sole responsibility of the fund manager. You have no say in this.

Money invested in share funds is not protected by any guarantees of either capital or performance, so choose wisely.

Property trusts are group investments in a property or group of properties and offer an easy way to get a foot in the real estate door. There is a wide choice of property trusts investing in residential, industrial, shopping malls and land, and this is one way of diversifying your property portfolio. These trusts usually have a stated policy of investing for growth with a potential for capital gain, or for income with a regular return. They are run by a managing company, and watched over by trustees. Unit holders are paid regularly by distributions from the earnings of the trust and your investment is secured by the properties it holds.

All property trusts produce a prospectus that sets out the aims and the expected growth and returns. Always read these thoroughly and seek advice if in doubt.

There are two types of property trusts: listed and unlisted. Listed property trusts are quoted on the ASX, so it is the market that values the units every day and you can follow their movements. Units are bought and sold through your stockbroker and transactions incur fees. As with all shares your money is available when you want it, at the market price. They are subject to market fluctuations but are not as volatile as some shares. These trusts are usually large and hold more than one property, although recent trends are leaning towards a single purpose trust such as a hotel trust formed to own and run a specific hotel.

Unlisted property trusts must be purchased from the fund manager through a prospectus application form. These trusts are becoming rare as more are seeking the advantages of listing. They directly own and manage real estate and the manager sets the value — it is not market driven. There is a front end charge and a long withdrawal time with extra fees. Always read the prospectus thoroughly and seek advice before committing yourself to this form of investment. All investors remember Estate Mortgage, one of the unlisted trust failures of the 1980s which cost many small investors their retirement nest egg.

Property syndicates These are occasionally advertised. They are not managed funds or trusts and joining one is rather like buying a share in a racehorse: you become a part owner of a particular property. A manager is chosen by the group to look after the finances and the property. Costs are low but access to your capital has to wait until all syndicate members agree to sell or take over your share. As always, be sure you know what you are stepping into.

Collectables

Collecting is not a fast way to make your fortune but it is fun. Mention Porsche, BMW, Patek Philippe, Cartier, Sidney Nolan or Chippendale and people's ears prick up! You need expertise for anything you collect if you are to make money at it. Great hoarders should investigate the boxes in the attic!

From art to matchboxes, anything is collectable and profitable, providing someone else will buy it. This is a very wide field. We collect frogs and cockatoos — no market but fun! The cups and saucers Grandma left can become heirlooms, or the stone figure at the bottom of the garden may turn out to be a famous artist's work. If you want to start your children on this path and give them something of value, collectables are more exciting than bonds!

However, collectables can take a long time to turn into cash. Many will do little more than hold their value. Some do not even manage that. Check the quantity made before you buy: keep in mind, the fewer produced, the higher the return. For example, rare Australian coins have outperformed many other investments over the past 30 years. Distinguishing marks and features or faults can all add value.

You must know your subject before setting out on this track. There are many reference books on all sorts of collectables, from hallmarks to names. Books themselves are a great collectable. If you have a complete set of first edition Enid Blyton, your bookshelf is holding a fortune!

The joy of owning something beautiful like artwork, furniture or even a vintage car can outweigh the 'maybe' monetary gain. Although necessary for insurance purposes, valuations are not worth the paper they are written on unless a buyer is waiting. Today's fad may not be tomorrow's choice!

If you enjoy visiting art galleries, why not keep your eyes peeled for a promising young artist's work. For a smallish investment you can begin your collection and enjoy living with it. It is fun to follow the growth of an artist and maybe you have chosen a future Picasso.

Antique furniture is a different kettle of fish. Be very careful, you could so easily make mistakes.

> **Peggy** Twenty years ago my son took me to an exhibition by a young artist. We both fell in love with his work and each bought a beautiful painting. Ten years later I sold mine at a profit of 350 per cent — those were the halcyon days of the late 1970s. To buy another of his works, I had to put my name on a waiting list — his talent had been recognised! This one now hangs in my lounge room and is not for sale.

Be aware that all collectables acquired after September 1985 are subject to Capital Gains Tax on any profit you make should you sell them.

Shares and real estate
Shares and real estate are two major investment alternatives and are dealt with in the next two chapters.

Keeping track
Keeping an accurate account of all your investments is essential in these high tax days. A register of your investments and a simple cashbook is all you need, until you have made millions. Then, of course, you'll pay someone else to do it for you!

7. SHARES

• • •

He who wishes to be rich in a day will be hanged in a year.
Leonardo da Vinci

Share the excitement, invest in the stock market, the place where the buying and selling of securities has been practised for over seven centuries. It's more interesting than other forms of investment because you can follow your money's daily movement, but it is a very volatile market. This is why the stock market is better suited for medium to long-term investments until you gain the confidence and knowledge to play the market.

> **Bits & Bytes**
> Stocks and bonds were first traded in Venice in 1262, when its government could not repay its temporary loans and converted them into bonds which could be traded in the market. In 1693 William III of England established the National Debt and the merchant brokers of the Royal Exchange traded bonds. The brokers did their business from Jonathan's Coffee House and in 1773 they named it the Stock Exchange.

WHY INVEST IN SHARES?

The aim of buying and selling shares is to make money. Their prices fluctuate in the short-term but grow or shrink in line with the state of our economy. Shares will give you income as well as capital growth if you buy wisely. Many of us do not understand the workings of this market or have been frightened off when there is a dramatic fall, such as happened in October 1987. Because we had faith in the stocks we had chosen, we held fast and have been rewarded with a dramatic growth in our portfolio. The lesson is: don't sell in a panic, most falls correct themselves and if you are in for the long haul have patience. History shows it will be rewarded. A loss is not a loss until you realise the asset — it is only a paper tiger!

Spending years Make these years the building blocks of your future and your fortune. Historically, shares grow, so these years are the ideal time to build a sound financial portfolio. They are also the speculative years when you can take a risk and maybe make a killing. If you fail, at least you have time to recoup and you'll have learned a few tricks on the way.

Growth years Consolidate, consolidate, consolidate. Buy new issues, floats, top-ups, in fact, buy as much as the budget can afford. Invest with caution, looking for stock that will return a regular income as well as growth because now you are building your long-term wealth.

Freedom years Now is the time to reap the benefits of a planned portfolio. Your shares should be flexible enough to sell in small parcels that can add income to your super. Buy with a view to selling at a profit and spend the proceeds on the things you've dreamed about.

INVESTING ON THE STOCK MARKET

The public float of companies like the Commonwealth Bank, Telstra, QANTAS and the NRMA has led to a better understanding of shares and how they work, dispelling the feeling that 'shares are not for me'. We no longer feel so intimidated by the thought of 'playing the market'. The number of ordinary Australians owning shares is rapidly increasing and more of us are managing our own investment and enjoy the mental exercise it demands.

Through the acquisition of shares by purchase, floats or inheritance you become a part owner of a company. The company uses your money, together with more from other individuals, institutions and loans for its expansion and development. As an investor you expect a return for the use of your money and this comes in several forms:

- Distribution of profits = dividends
- An increase in share prices = capital growth
- The issue of 'bonus' shares = extra free shares
- The offer of 'rights' to buy, usually at a discount = extra shares

To purchase shares you need a stockbroker, either by dealing directly with a broker or through your financial adviser/planner. Stockbrokers are licensed by the Australian Stock Exchange (ASX) to trade on the market and they are the only people permitted to trade.

Bits & Bytes

In 1828 Matthew Gregson started as a dealer in shares and failed. In 1835 William Barton, the father of Australia's first Prime Minister, established himself as an 'agent for the transfer of shares'. In 1987 the six separate stock exchanges in Australia amalgamated to form the Australian Stock Exchange Limited, our national stock market.

THE AUSTRALIAN STOCK EXCHANGE (ASX)

The Australian Stock Exchange is the link between companies requiring money and people who have money to invest. It provides the marketplace for the continual buying and selling of shares. It is the market in which stocks and bonds are resold on a recurring basis. The performance of the market, directly or indirectly, affects all of us. By investing in shares we are investing in Australia and its future.

Around 1,500 companies have their stocks listed on the Australian Stock Exchange. These companies operate in many fields, including mining, manufacturing, agriculture, chemicals, tourism, health, financial services, build homes and shopping centres, and exports. All are the core of our free enterprise system and are responsible for the economic growth of this country and for the creation of jobs.

The ASX is subject to regulation by the Australian Securities and Investments Commission (ASIC), a government body responsible for overseeing the Corporations Law. The ASX is a single organisation with offices in each state capital city, all connected by a computerised trading system known as SEATS (the Stock Exchange Automated Trading System). It is the market place for the trading of shares, government bonds and other fixed interest securities — an auction house with buyers and sellers bidding against each other, through their broker, with the price being determined by supply and demand.

SEATS was fully operational in September 1990, and provides one national market and one national price for stock. Trading is now immediate, which means first in first served. Gone are the hectic days of blackboards and coloured jackets on the stock exchange floor. Trading now occurs on the screen in the broker's office and the client can stay on the phone while the transaction takes place. The terminal screen uses colour for quick recognition — blue for buyers, yellow for sellers, red for falling prices and light green for rising prices. This program is a world first.

To make it easier to follow the movement of trading more accurately, the ASX, in association with Standard and Poor's, has established several indices within the Exchange. It has expanded the first index, the All Ordinaries (All Ords) to include 500 companies (up from 251) to give a 99 per cent assessment of the value of our market. The S&P/ASX 100, S&P/ASX 200 and the S&P/ASX 300 indices have also been added to the share market reports. These listings show the movement as well as the capitalisation within the market, which will give investors another benchmark and more information. The All Ords is the one to watch until you become very specialised.

All companies listed must follow the rules of the ASX and they must notify the Exchange of anything that could affect the price of their shares. Brokers have a trust account into which all clients' money must be deposited and this account is audited each year. Any discrepancy can lead to the cancellation of the broker's licence.

Insider trading is viewed as a serious offence by the ASX and the ASIC. If a trader uses inside confidential information about a stock to buy or sell before the information becomes public knowledge, he or she has contravened the law and could end up in jail. This is considered an offence throughout the world.

Bits & Bytes
Remember Nick Gleeson, who used his 'inside' knowledge to play the market with Barings' money and brought that well-respected company down.

ADVANTAGES OF INVESTING IN SHARES
Accessibility Shares are easy to buy and sell. The ASX operates every working day and your orders are executed immediately. This gives you a wonderful sense of security over other forms of investment. If you have a sudden emergency, you can have money within three working days. There are no large exit charges only the brokerage. If you have a windfall you can be a shareholder taking part in growth and profits within three days. Again, there are no entry fees, only brokerage. Amounts as small as $500 can be invested — so can your millions!

Capital growth By careful selection of growth companies you can increase your capital slowly and surely. A portfolio geared to growth and income takes time to show results. If you have the nerve to speculate, you may become a millionaire or a pauper overnight.

Buybacks These alter the composition of a portfolio. They reflect the aim of companies to repay shareholders for their loyalty. In these days of off shore operations where there is no imputation credit, a buyback gives the investor cash in return for all or part of their holding, at the same time increasing the value of the remaining shares. There can be tax advantages, so read the fine print that comes with the offer and do your sums.

New issues When a company requires more funds, it offers new shares at a discount price without any charges, This increases the number of shareholders on the company's register and might mean the dividend is thinner on the ground, but it increases your holding. Companies have to state dividend intentions at the time they announce the issue.

Rights issues This is an offer of the right to purchase (either now or some time in the future). a set number of shares in ratio to your holding. The price is usually lower than the market price and there are no charges. These rights can be sold on the market.

Dividends These are all yours, paid out of the company's profits, promulgated as cents per share and usually paid every six months. There are no management fees and if they are fully franked you get a tax advantage which other forms of investment do not offer.

Dividend Imputation In 1987 the Federal Government introduced dividend imputation making shares an attractive investment alternative by removing double taxation. The company still pays tax, at the company rate, and the shareholder is given a credit for this against the tax they have to pay. Dividends are listed as fully franked, partially franked or unfranked.

Loan security This involves using your shareholding as security for a loan. CHESS is causing some problems in this field so we suggest you check this before applying. There are several options available.

Fringe benefits These are rather like mileage points given by the airlines. Some companies give their shareholders perks and discounts. You could have free nights in company hotels, discounts on shopping and car repairs, free theatre tickets, free safety deposit facilities and even 'free lunches'!

Wise investors do not look at short-term movements. They concentrate on the fundamentals of the company such as market share, earnings, management, research and development, and are always aware of long-term growth. The longer money is invested in the market, the greater the potential for growth, so long as you have bought into growth companies, not speculative ones or fly-by-nighters.

Ideally, shares should be bought using your budget's 10 per cent savings. A lottery win could tempt you to try a few specs but remember if they go under, the shareholder is the last to be paid.

BE AN INFORMED INVESTOR
Have a clear vision of what you want from this form of investment, be informed and seek the advice of your stockbroker. Keep these key points in mind:
- Invest for the medium to long term — it's a volatile market and you need to invest for five years or more to really reap the benefits.
- Balance your portfolio — by diversifying. Buy a range of shares from a variety of areas. A balanced portfolio should include stock from the banking, retail and service industries as well as from mining, finance and media areas.
- Focus on the top 100 to 200 companies when making your choice. These are the companies that account for a large percentage of the daily market turnover. Their returns are usually more reliable than those of smaller companies.
- 'Blue chip' companies, the established ones, tend to be less volatile, increasing at a steady rate over the years but their annual returns are often slightly lower.

- Look for value and quality. Analyse the balance sheet and future business prospects. Good management is a key factor in performance, so keep an eye on the CEOs.
- Buy, sell or hold? The market goes in cycles and knowing where you are in the cycle is the hard bit. Ideally, you buy low and sell high.

The thing that frightens people about the stock market is the way it changes so rapidly. If you didn't know better you'd swear it had a mind of its own. A close look will show you that these daily fluctuations are shaped by many factors: government policy, balance of payments, taxation changes, international markets, company management, economic conditions, industrial action, impending legal action and interest rates but over the years the pattern tends to be an upwards one.

> Interest rates up = shares down
> Interest rates down = shares up

Bits & Bytes
ASX records indicate that the number of women holding shares has increased enormously since 1991. This is attributed to the large floats such as Woolworths and the Commonwealth Bank.

The two main categories listed on the ASX are (1) industrial shares, and (2) the resources section (mining and oil). These in turn are subdivided further. Industrials cover industries such as manufacturing, finance, retailing, tourism and health. Mining and oil shares are considered to have a greater risk due to the uncertainty of exploration and the fluctuation of world commodities and oil prices.

Ordinary shares The most common form of share ownership, they offer the benefits of dividend distributions paid out of net profits, voting rights at AGMs and participation in the growth of the company with bonus or rights issues. Ordinary shareholders rank last in priority if a company is wound up.

Preference shares These are similar to ordinary shares, but have a fixed rate of dividend which must be paid before the ordinary dividends. If a company is wound up these shares have preference over ordinary shares. There are different types of preferences:
- Non-cumulative rank before ordinary shares for each dividend.
- Cumulative accumulate the dividends when they are not paid.
- Participating have a priority right to further profits.
- Redeemable are redeemed on an agreed date at par value.
- Convertible are converted to ordinary shares on a fixed date.

Convertible notes They offer the best of both worlds by giving a stipulated income and a share investment. They are a loan to the company at a fixed rate of interest for a set time, after which they convert into ordinary shares or cash.

Contributing shares These are partly paid, and when the company requires a future payment, the shareholder is obliged to meet the 'call' from the company, which can be for all or part of the monies outstanding.

Bonus issue This is a free issue of shares to shareholders, and usually reflect any increase in the company's assets. They are issued in ratio to the number of shares already held (one new share for every five). For capital gains tax purposes, these issues 'grandfather back' (revert) to the price paid for the original shares.

Rights These are an offer to a shareholder to buy new shares in the company, usually below the current market price. Like bonus issues, they are allocated in ratio to the number held. They can be traded on the ASX and are listed separately in the stock reports.

Dividend Reinvestment Plan (DRP) Instead of receiving a cash dividend, the shareholder opts to purchase additional shares in the company, usually at a discount off the market price. No brokerage or stamp duty is payable. CGT comes into play if you sell your DRP.

Float Floats are the initial raising of capital by public subscription. A prospectus is issued setting out the company's objectives and senior officers. It gives a forecast of earnings and must be approved by the ASIC and be acceptable to the ASX. These are worth considering as there is no brokerage payable and you are entering a developing company (you hope!).

Takeover When a company wishes to take control of another it, the bidder, offers existing shareholders a price per share, shares in the new company or a combination of both. Again, no extra charges but remember that if you accept a takeover offer you are selling your original holding.

Derivatives, Futures, Options and Warrants This is a specialised and complex area operated and controlled by the ASX. You need expert advice before investing in this market and should only enter this field when you understand its complexities. It is not a place for the faint hearted. Some give the buyer or seller the right to buy or sell at an agreed price at a set time in the future, others give the trader the option to do so.

BUYING AND SELLING

When you direct your broker to buy or sell, you are entering into a binding contract with him. Make sure your requirements are clear, repeat them and keep notes of your instructions to avoid any misunderstanding. There are several ways you can ask your broker to buy or sell:

At best Sometimes called at discretion, which means the broker fulfils your order at his discretion.

At market Your broker buys or sells at whatever market price is current when you place your order.

At limit Your order will be executed within the limits you set. Orders are executed via SEATS, which is the ASX Automated Trading System. Your order is entered on your broker's terminal and processed in order of receipt regardless of the size of the request. Big players don't have priority over small players.

Brokers need access to funds, so you need to set up a client trading account to facilitate the transfer of funds for buying and selling. We use a CMT account with our broking firm.

Shares are bought and sold in multiples, making up a marketable parcel. Small numbers, once referred to as an odd lot, perhaps acquired through dividend reinvestment, are now grouped together before sale.

All orders between you and your broker are due for settlement on T+3 (transaction plus three days). You will receive a contract note telling you what price the shares were at the time of sale or purchase, plus brokerage fees and government charges, if applicable. Both the buyer and the seller pay these fees. Keep all the contract notes safely as they are essential records for assessing CGT on sales.

It is possible, but difficult, to buy and sell shares privately or 'off market'. You have to find a buyer or seller willing to trade this way (usually between family members), You need to instruct your Clearing House Electronic Subregister System (CHESS) sponsor to transfer the shares to the buyer or to convert those shares on to the issuer-sponsored subregister. You then have to fill in an Australian Standard Transfer form and pay the necessary charges. There are no brokerage fees but it does involve some running around.

Internet trading

Knowledge of the market is essential and this is not an area for the beginner or the nervous trader. Read the brochures carefully before committing yourself, check the fees, then sign up with a supplier and establish a trading account.

You can sit at your computer, access your online broker and your order is immediately placed on the market. You are buying or selling at the market price at that instant. There can be technological hiccups, so if you are one of the 'mission critical traders' you may need a backup system. All trading is done via CHESS and your broker will send a contract note of the transaction by mail or email.

Bits & Bytes
Frog Focus is an ASX program involving the community in frog conservation, in partnership with zoos and acquaria across Australia. Leap into ASX Frog Focus www.asxfrogfocus.com.

CHESS

Clearing House Electronic Subregister System — CHESS. This is a clearing 'house' for all trading transactions and is the electronic subregister for all ASX listed companies. Now that all ASX transfers and settlements are done electronically, the whole process is fast, secure, efficient and cost-effective.

You have two choices when having your ownership in a company recorded. You can either stay with the issuing company, or you sign with a sponsoring broker.

If you nominate to stay with the company issuing the securities as your sponsor on a share subregister, you will be allocated a Security-holder Reference Number (SRN) and will have a different SRN for each company.

If you decide to go with CHESS, you sign a sponsorship agreement with your broker who then does the buying and selling of your shares. You will be given a Holder Identification Number (HIN) to quote before your broker will trade on your behalf. This agreement is a legal document which sets out terms and conditions.

By signing with a sponsoring broker you are virtually limiting yourself to dealing through one broker for all your share transactions. You can use another broker but it may cost you extra fees and time. Ask your broker to explain CHESS in full, or consult the ASX's excellent brochure.

A statement of your holding in each company and of any sale or purchase which changes your holdings is issued regularly.

If you are using your financial adviser/planner or bank to buy and sell, they will have an agreement with a stockbroker and will forward all holding statements. Keep these important records of your portfolio.

KEEPING TRACK

Records are essential, particularly in these days of Capital Gains Tax (CGT) You will need a register of holdings and a cashbook. Use the register to record details of the purchase and sale, prices paid or received, fees, other expenses involved, and any information you need to keep. All identification numbers are best kept here. This information is essential if you sell your shares and become liable for CGT.

Use your cashbook to record all income which includes imputation credits, value of bonus shares and dividend re-investments. Your share register and cashbook are the most important part of your filing system — keep them up-to-date.

Bits & Bytes
Bulls and Bears: a bull tosses the prices up, a bear claws the market down. These terms are constantly in use in stock markets worldwide.

Once you understand the workings of the share market, it becomes a challenge to beat the experts. Before buying into this market, try running a 'fantasy' portfolio over a couple of months to build a good grasp of what you want.

Another option is to join an Investment Club. These clubs, now gaining worldwide popularity, are based on the Beardstown Ladies, a group of American women who got together to improve their knowledge of the share market. Subscriptions were pooled and each one followed a particular stock for a month. Each month they met to discuss their findings and vote on club purchases. They ended up with a portfolio that outperformed the market by a large percentage. This kind of club does need to have a sound and easily understood legal structure.

DIVIDEND IMPUTATION AND CAPITAL GAINS TAX
Dividend imputation

The Australian Government's decision in 1987 to introduce dividend imputation made investing in the share market more attractive. Before its introduction, a company paid tax on its profit and the shareholder paid a second time on the dividends declared from that post-tax profit — this was double taxation.

Dividend imputation, also called 'franking', is the rebate you are credited with on franked dividends and is an essential part of your equation when deciding which shares to purchase. A franking credit is noted on the dividend advice note. This can be fully franked, partially franked or unfranked, which reflects the amount of tax already paid by the company. You must keep all dividend advice notes because they are your record of tax credits and are vital for when tax return time comes around. The advice note will show: the dividend rate per share; number of shares; franked amount; unfranked amount; imputation credit and; dividend actually paid to you.

On tax returns you must state the total dividend, including the imputation credit. You therefore need a column in the cashbook where you add the amount of the cheque to the imputation credit, giving you a gross amount received. The imputation credit is shown as a deduction later in the tax return form. If your overall tax bill is lower than your imputation credits you will pay no tax and get a refund. If you are liable for tax on other sources of income, the imputation credits can help pay that tax.

Although more and more of our companies are moving overseas, the income they earn there does not as yet attract imputation credits. Therefore dividend 'tax paid' credits are reduced. If a reciprocal tax agreement between the relevant governments exists, you will receive a 'withholding tax' credit.

Capital Gains Tax

This is a prime reason for keeping accurate and complete records of all investments. Your cashbooks should show each investment's value at the time of acquisition, including all costs that are relevant: commission, brokerage, government charges, and details of bonus shares, DRP and rights. Records of the price received and costs of selling are needed for assessing CGT. Without these records you or your accountant will have to spend time finding these details when you sell shares or any investment at a profit or a loss. Keep all documentation received from your broker and the company.

THE ARITHMETIC OF SHARES

> I only took a regular course ...
> the different branches of Arithmetic —
> Ambition, Distraction, Uglification and Derision
> *Lewis Carroll*

Do your sums. All you need are the four basic skills of arithmetic — addition, subtraction, multiplication and division. A simple calculator will do the lot very easily! Every few months you should assess the performance of your share portfolio to decide if you need to buy, sell or add some new blood. The daily market report, the All Ordinaries Index (All Ords), published in major newspapers and on the Internet, will give you the current sales and returns of the Australian Stock Exchange for all areas of the market.

When comparing your overall dividend return with your property or money market investments, allow for the fact that the share dividend you have received, if fully or partially franked, will have a built-in tax credit. This increases the returns from shares over other investments.

Your tax file number should be quoted to your CHESS broker or sponsor company. Otherwise the highest rate of tax will be deducted from all dividend payments. If you do not wish to supply your TFN you will have to wait until your next tax return to claim any excess paid against tax due.

The All Ords is a statistical measure of the market performance of all listed companies. This is a means of showing, in shorthand, what is happening to our shares. The All Ords commenced at midnight on 31 December 1979 with a base of 500 points.

Follow the movement of your share portfolio and keep track of your climb to that first million! The ASX listings gives detailed information and, unless you are playing the market full time, the following will help you find out all you need to know:

52-week high/low This is a guide to the share's long-term performance showing the highest and lowest price for the period.

Day's high/low Just what it says.

Vol 100s This term indicates the pattern of movement on that day. Could it be a 'run'?

Div yield % This is calculated daily by dividing the annual dividend per share by the share price, expressed as a percentage which shows the theoretical return on a share purchased on that day. It is a good way to compare the return from each stock.

Div c per share It shows the dividend, in cents, received over the last year for each share. An 'f' or 'p' after the amount indicates a fully or partially franked dividend.

Grossed up yield % This percentage includes notional benefits from franking credits. It gives the best overall picture to quickly assess your gross return.

P/E ratio All advisers use this term. It is simply the daily price of an ordinary share divided by the annual earning per share. It indicates whether a share is under or over priced.

The Australian economy is influenced by overseas factors including the rise and fall of the overseas indices. The big ones are the Dow Jones in New York, the FTSE 100 in London, the DAX in Berlin and the Nikkei in Tokyo. The world's stock exchanges work on the same principles as the ASX.

Bits & Bytes
The Dow Jones Index was started late last century by Mr Dow and Mr Jones with 11 stocks. It is now based on 65 blue chip US stock in three areas, industrial, transport and utilities.

Success with picking a stable portfolio is achieved if you can spend a lot of time analysing movements in the market. Bargain hunting can be dangerous unless you set yourself a buying or selling limit. For a long-term investor, most of the daily rises and falls in the market become irrelevant after 5-10 years.

READY-MADE PORTFOLIOS
Ready-made portfolios are not trusts or pooled funds. They are recent innovations now being offered by banks and investment houses. You buy a ready-made portfolio of blue chip shares as a set

package for as little as $3,000 and you can add to them. The price quoted on your first inquiry is a close approximate only as the shares vary from day to day. The small charges are calculated on the cost of the transaction. You can sell all or part of this portfolio at any time and brokerage is a small amount. You become a real shareholder, receiving annual reports and attending shareholder meetings.

Ready-made portfolios are a great way to get your portfolio up and running if you are short of time. Research thoroughly before parting with cash.

Learning more

The Australian Stock Exchange offers excellent courses in most capital cities. The courses range from a simple introduction to the share market to the really advanced stuff. You can choose to attend lectures at the ASX or learn at home via either online or the old fashioned method of correspondence.

The ASX holds regular talks in its offices, on different aspects of the market. ASX Investor Hours are usually organised for lunch hours or after work. ASX Open Day, is an all day event usually held on a weekend, and is well worth attending. Leading brokers and investment companies attend. You can pick up all sorts of brochures, hear experts speak and ask questions.

Bits & Bytes
If the market sounds excited about an investment — you're probably too late. Twenty stocks gives you a good spread.

8. REAL ESTATE

• • •

> They're not making any more land.
> *Will Rogers*

Women are now a force to be reckoned within the world of real estate. Many women have realised that to buy well and add value to property is one of the best ways to secure financial independence and that a home can be the beginning of a property portfolio. The earlier you start the better the resulting security, and it is a good form of compulsory saving. Your first house teaches you the principles as well as the catches of buying and negotiating. With the first sale, other new skills are quickly acquired.

Real estate is an interesting and an essential part of any portfolio. The main attraction is that it is a tangible asset. Its land content is indestructible and you can insure against the threat of fire. Historically, real estate has shown that it is safer than most other forms of investment in times of recession. Companies can go under and shares can drop dramatically, though they will rise again over time but for some investors this can be a nerve-racking wait. Artwork and other collectables can go out of favour, but land is always there and bricks and mortar will last. You can choose the time to buy and sell and you are not so vulnerable to other people's whims or panics.

Property is a long-term investment. It can be your home, an investment property or both together. Your home can be more than a roof over your head, particularly if you improve and add to it. Remember, your home is exempt from Capital Gains Tax. The ideal situation is to use your home as a security and take out a loan to buy the next property. That makes both properties work for you, building an asset and returning you income at the same time. For security, capital growth and a steady income return, real estate is hard to beat. You can also enter this market through listed or unlisted property trusts, a great way to start small.

According to the Australian Bureau of Statistics, almost 80 per cent of us will retire with less than $8,000 per year and more than 60 per cent will retire with a lump sum of less than $20,000. Only 6 per cent will have a real estate portfolio and, of those, less than 0.2 per cent will own more than five investment properties. Investment in real estate can be your own retirement nest-egg.

Bricks and mortar do the same as any investment — the earlier you start the more you will make. The longer you are in a market the more your capital can grow. One point worth remembering is that a mortgage payment is an enforced form of saving, you are less likely to fritter away any spare cash.

For young women especially, the real estate world is your oyster — open it and find the pearl!

Spending Years When the joy of independence is still new, some of us start off sharing a rented house, dashing about and having fun. However, this is the best time in your life to save hard and get your foot in the real estate door. Of course, if you decide to have a family, housing takes on an air of urgency.

Growth Years The needs and demands have changed. Is it time to house-hunt or is it better to go upwards or sideways? Proceed with care — if you extend, overcapitalisation is a danger. You may need room for teenagers, or an elderly parent. You may just want your own place.

The best of all positions occurs when you can retain your first property, having paid off the mortgage, and use this one as security for the next. Rent it and let the rent pay the mortgage, once it is under, control consider a second rental property. Don't stop at two places — make them work towards the third and even a fourth.

Freedom Years You're free of mortgages at last, and income is rolling in from the other properties. The kids have gone, so look for a smaller place with every comfort you can imagine. Now you can sell the odd property to finance overseas trips, a new car or help the children if needed. It's also the time to spend your children's inheritance.

Warning — borrowing on your house for luxuries, such a holiday, and adding the cost to your mortgage is an expensive option. Calculate the extra interest you will pay over the years. It could be better to borrow at a higher daily rate of interest on your credit card, or take out a personal loan. It's worth taking the time to do the sums.

RENTING

To buy or to rent? A mortgage will reduce your disposable income, and that scares most people. It represents a huge responsibility. There are pros and cons for both options and the decision will depend on your financial position.

When renting, you have to find the money for a bond, usually equal to one month's rent, as well as finding the rent to cover the first few weeks. Deposits will be required for the utilities and, of course, you may need to purchase or hire any furniture you require. The bond is safely held in a trust account and is refunded on the termination of your lease, less any outstanding monies you owe or cost of repairs that can be laid at your door. Make sure your budget includes the regular payments of rent.

Each state has a government department that takes care of any problems that may arise. Look for it in the phonebook or ask the renting agent. You have rights and obligations and so does the landlord — make sure you are aware of them.

Rent money is 'dead' money but at least it is easier to move from a rented place and you have no repairs and maintenance, no council rates or strata levies to pay. Hopefully you are saving and building your other assets.

Compare the amount you are paying in rent with the cost of servicing a mortgage, always remembering that the money you are paying into the mortgage represents an asset that will be free of Capital Gains Tax when or if you sell.

Renting is a wonderful way to begin your research into areas in which you would like to buy property. By living in a district, you can watch the rise and fall of values, a very important part of research for home and investment. There was a time when real estate could be considered a lottery in which everyone held a winning ticket. Now we need to carefully assess where and what to buy, values differ so much. A water view adds incalculable dollars to the price and an inner city car space can be worth as much as the suburban house.

Whatever your personal choice, there is great satisfaction and security in owning your own place, adding to it and improving it.

BUYING REAL ESTATE

The advantages of buying property are many. Paying the mortgage starts you on the track of compulsory saving a good credit rating which will stand you in good stead when you apply for a loan for your first real estate venture. This is your home for as long as you choose. You can decorate or change it as much as you like and can afford. You can't be told to move out or have the rent raised unexpectedly. Remember, though, that interest rates, council and water rates can all rise.

The hunt is on! You've worked out how much you can afford to borrow — start looking. Everyone will offer their pet theory on when, where and how to buy — the market's up (or down), shares are up (or down), employment is up (or down). In fact, something will always be going the wrong way. Weigh it all up and make up your own mind. As long as you know your price range and can afford the repayments, you are ready to start hunting.

The media, real estate agents, word-of-mouth and legwork all help you make the choice. List the pros and cons of each place you think worth a second look and take this each time you go looking.

Never be hurried by pushy salespeople. Remember this is a huge investment — it's your money and you are in charge.

This first purchase should be considered a part of your overall investment strategy.

THE EXTRA COSTS

The stated purchase price is one thing, the actual price you end up paying before you take possession is another. The extra costs can be considerable and may make the dream house you have just found unobtainable. These costs vary according to the price of the property, the number of experts you consult and the state in which you are purchasing. Whether buying a house, a unit, a townhouse or a block of land as a home or an investment, the costs are much the same and include the following:

Building inspection

This is a necessity before you buy — you never know what is hidden by a coat of paint or piece of hardboard. Your inspector should give you a detailed report of any defects such as rising damp or illegal extensions. The report should include an estimate of the cost of any repairs. White ants can also be a problem, so ask for a pest inspection and make sure you get a written report. If there have been any alterations or new work to the structure, it is advisable to secure a copy of any certificates approving the work. You can then decide if this house is worth chasing.

Legal and conveyancing costs

These expenses are your safeguard as they include checking the contract of sale, making sure there are no problems with the title deeds or any appendages, such as a caveat (which can limit what you can do with the property). Checking all documents is essential so you know if there are illegal structures, debts, strata title special levies coming up, rights of ways — in fact, anything that will affect your use of the property or cost you extra money. These checks should be done by a lawyer or a registered conveyancer, but not someone suggested by the seller. You need an impartial assessment.

What is an 'option'?
The vendor may give you an option to purchase. This is a legal document that stipulates a set time for you to make a decision. The price paid for an option normally forms a part of the purchase price if you decide to buy. If you do not go ahead you lose this option fee. In other words, you pay a fee to reserve the property for yourself for a period and the vendor cannot sell it while you hold that option.

A holding deposit
A percentage of the purchase price is paid during negotiations as a measure of good faith, indicating your interest in buying the property. It is paid before the exchange of contracts but is not a guarantee of a sale, and is repayable if a contract is not entered into.

Establishment fees
This fee is payable when you submit your loan application to the lender. They cover the mortgagee's valuation fees, legal and administration costs.

Government fees
These vary from state to state and according to the value of the property. Stamp duty may be payable on the property transfer and the mortgage documents. There is also a government fee for registering the transfer of title and the mortgage.

Insurance
Several types of insurance are necessary, including mortgage insurance and building insurance. Premiums are based on the amount insured, the level of cover you choose and the type of insurance. Mortgage insurance (to cover the lender) may also be required.

Rates and other adjustments

You may have to reimburse the vendor a portion of any payments already made for council and water rates or strata title levies paid in advance by the vendor.

Bits & Bytes

An eccentric American millionaire, Sara Winchester, had a theory that she would die if she stopped building her house. For 38 years she kept adding rooms. When she did die, her Californian mansion contained 160 rooms (some only a few centimetres wide), 10,000 windows (many opened on to blank walls) and dozens of staircases leading nowhere!

BUYING

You can buy property at auction, through an agent, by private sale, or you can buy 'off the plan'.

Buying at auction

When you find the house you like for sale at auction, ask the agent what price it is expected to reach. This will only be an estimation and the actual price may be higher or lower on the day of the auction. Set yourself a firm price and be careful not to get carried away with the excitement of the bidding. Keep your cool and stick to your maximum price.

Before the auction ask your solicitor or conveyancer to check the title documents, contract and all documents relating to the property. If it is in a declared heritage area, you may not be able to paint it the colour of your choice. If strata titled, look at the minutes of the owners' council meetings for signs of ongoing or upcoming problems and expenses in the block. These checks are an added expense so take them into account when setting your bidding limit. They have to be paid whether you are successful or not — but you need to know before you bid that all is as it seems.

From personal experience we suggest you attend several

auctions. Watch the body language — it is fascinating and can tell you a lot. You may learn to judge who is prepared to go the limit and who will drop out if you suddenly double the previous bid.

The reserve price at auctions is the lowest price the vendor will accept and this is kept secret. The vendor is entitled to one bid and can try to 'run' the price, be aware of this. If the bidding doesn't reach the reserve the property is 'passed in'. If your bid is successful you are legally committed to the purchase and you must pay a deposit, usually 10 per cent, and sign the contract then and there. A bid made without your finance arrangements in place may not be accepted by the auctioneer.

If the property is passed in below the reserve price, private negotiations often take place, with the highest bidder having the first opportunity to make an offer.

Buying through an agent or by private treaty

Buying properties through an agent or direct from the vendor is less nerve racking than bidding at an auction but the adrenalin doesn't flow nearly as fast! Agents handle negotiations with the vendor, answer your questions regarding the property, supply you with the contract of sale and accept the deposit, which they hold on trust until the completion of the sale. Agents are paid a commission by the vendor. The buyer pays no agent's fees.

When you buy direct from the vendor, they supply the contract and sale details. In this case, you do need your solicitor or conveyancer from the word go. The vendor is saving commission, so the price should be lower. Checks of recent sales in that area need to be made to make certain the price is realistic.

Buying off the plan

In this case, the building offered for sale is only at the planning stage or is only partly built. You are shown a plan or perhaps a model and you pay a deposit with completion of payment at a set date. You cannot lock in a loan until final settlement and if the loan company's valuation comes in lower than you expected it's a nasty shock so get an expert to read the contract. This is not the time for DIY conveyancing.

Buying off the plan is a common way to buy into new unit complexes. The developer usually constructs a demonstration unit at the site. This gives you an idea of how the finished unit will look and the quality of the white goods. Often the buyer is offered a choice of wall and carpet colours. If the developer goes to the wall before completion you could be in trouble.

Once you are advised of settlement day, arrange an inspection of the property, list any defects and things you want corrected. Instruct your solicitor not to settle until these defects are attended to. Once the developer has your money you have less chance of getting things done!

That deposit you paid all that time ago (ours was actually a 3-year wait) is held in the developer's trust account and the interest earned is split between the buyer and the seller on settlement.

No matter how you buy — auction, agent, private sale or off the plan — once the contract of sale has been signed, you and the vendor are bound by it and you can both enforce it. Settlement day varies by mutual consent, and your solicitor or conveyancer will represent you. It is essential to check that the property is just as you bought it, with all inclusions.

Always have a pre-settlement inspection. At one property we purchased, we found the vendor's old dog abandoned, unfed for a week. We fed it and contacted our solicitor who refused to settle until the dog was fed and removed to a new home.

FINDING THE MONEY

The housing loan business has become very competitive and it is no longer the exclusive field of the banks, so shop around and read the fine print. Research well done is worth all the time you put into it. Your ability to finance the purchase and service the loan is vital to your success and survival.

Where do you start? The best place is probably the bank that has your accounts, credit cards and any other loans. It may not be your final choice but it will lead you into the complexities of mortgage finance and the costs. This first foray will give you an idea of the questions to ask as you visit other lenders. There are now many non-banking institutions anxious to give you a home loan, so watch the papers for their advertisements.

The deposit for a house is usually 10 per cent and 80 per cent seems to be the figure most lenders will advance for the principal. Without mortgage insurance, this leaves you to find another 10 per cent. As a rule of thumb, 25 per cent of your gross income is considered the maximum amount you need to set aside to pay the mortgage.

Paperwork now smothers you. The first step is to get the necessary forms and then have at least the following information at your fingertips to make the approval of your loan run smoothly and quickly:

- Personal identification — passport, driver's licence, credit cards
- Details of the property, including the contract of sale
- The name of your solicitor or conveyancer
- Details of income — substantiated by your group certificate or tax assessment.
- Other assets such as life assurance/super, investments, cash, car etc
- Any financial commitments — credit cards, hire purchase, outstanding loans
- Details of living expenses to give an idea of your monthly costs.

The options are overwhelming. There are base variable rates, standard variable rates, guaranteed rates, fixed interest rates and a raft of others — the terminology is only restricted by the provider's imagination! Everything seems to change every week. Your final decision must be based on a sound assessment of your ability to service the loan. If you are partway through a loan and you decide to transfer your mortgage, there could be costs incurred that make it uneconomical to change.

Paying weekly or fortnightly is better than monthly if you can manage it in your budget. The more frequently you make your mortgage payments, the sooner the property becomes yours. You pay less interest thus reducing the overall cost.

Early payout
This option may arise, for example, if you suddenly receive a large bonus or an inheritance. If this happens, negotiate an early exit clause before signing the contract. Bear in mind that altering your mortgage always involves extra legal and government costs. It may be to your financial advantage to keep the mortgage going for its full term and use the windfall in other investments. Watch for this and do your maths.

Other options
Sometimes options allow you to make extra repayments, so you can pay your loan off faster, hence saving interest. Others will let you 'redraw' or use any principal you may have repaid over and above the original loan. Again, there will be costs but it gives you access to the money if you need it.

Bridging finance
It provides just that: a financial bridge to help you if you have to sell your present house to finance another one. It normally has a higher interest rate and is available from traditional lenders.

Securitisation
Another new word to be added to your dictionary. This is an investment tool used by institutions on property loans. These offer very competitive conditions and interest rates. The mortgagee bundles mortgages into large parcels and turns this parcel into a loan investment vehicle with the face value of all the mortgages as security. This parcel is then sold to a third party at a lower rate than that which the mortgagors are paying.

The buyer of the parcel supplies the money while the original mortgagee or middle man is the securitisor. The end user, the mortgagor, usually benefits by paying a lower interest rate on the loan. The risk of loan defaulters is minimal as it is spread over a large number of mortgagors. Securitisation is now being used to buy many types of investments, including shares.

The second time round with your property portfolio will be easier. You have an established 'track record', so it is important not to default on a payment without notifying your mortgagee.

Checking your annual home loan statements can be a nightmare as errors can be made in calculations. There are software program available which make it easy.

TITLES: THE PROOF OF OWNERSHIP
Torrens Title
In this system, the proof of ownership rests on one document only, and each transfer of ownership is registered in the Lands Department. Sir Robert Torrens devised this system of recording ownership in 1858, when issuing grants of land in South Australia. It was so successful that it was quickly adopted by the rest of Australia, replacing the Old Systems Title. Today this system, or others based on it, are used throughout the world.

Strata Title
This is a form of Torrens Title commonly used for home units, townhouses and other forms of group housing. It divides the land and the building into separate lots and designates the common areas. Each owner is a member of the Owners' Corporation and has a separate certificate of title. The common property is used and owned by the Owners' Corporation which acts as agent for the members. When the original plan was registered with the Lands Department each unit was allocated voting rights according to the size and perceived value of the lot.

Strata title living gives you individuality within a semi-community life. For women alone it provides good security, and sometimes companionship. It can take a lot of hassles out of home owning — fixing of a leaking roof or a broken window is just a phone call away. There are many booklets put out by government departments explaining the ins and outs of strata living. We have enjoyed strata living for nearly 30 years.

Company Title

In this case the whole building is owned by a company and you should be aware that you are not buying real estate: you are buying shares in a company that owns real estate. The shareholders have control over who buys, who rents and how the building is maintained. It is often hard to resell or obtain a loan because the security is in shares rather than in real estate, though this is becoming less restrictive as lending bodies proliferate. Before you buy, ask to see the company's articles of association. You must know exactly what your rights would be before parting with your investment dollars.

INVESTMENT PROPERTIES

Investing in property is a different ball game to owning your own home, although both represent a step to building wealth. It requires careful research, especially into the best way to raise and service the finance you need. Even if you haven't paid off your home, it can be used as collateral to raise money for the first investment property. The rent should go a long way to meeting the mortgage payments so don't be afraid of the debt you are incurring. Just make sure your figures are right and that you have allowed for unforeseen circumstances. Mortgage insurance is worth considering.

Negative gearing involves borrowing more than the income earned by the investment. It is a very useful as a long-term wealth building strategy that. As long as it is well managed, it will enhance your portfolio. It deducts expenses, including interest payments, from other income and builds a tax benefit. Be wary, though, as it can be deceptively easy to overextend.

Buying property is not only for the young and middle aged. We have bought and sold property in our Freedom years, though we do feel that starting young is an advantage.

It is a misconception that you need lots of money to start if you have gone some way towards paying off your home. What you do need is the deposit plus all those costs relating to the purchase and an assurance by your mortgagee that they will lend you the money. There is fierce competition between the traditional lenders — banks and building societies — and the new group of mortgage providers such as insurance and financial investment companies. Shop around for the one that suits you the best. Do not over-extend yourself — make sure you can service the loan and still have a safety net for those unexpected hiccups life throws at us.

The most important decisions are: where and what you should buy. House or unit? New or dilapidated? Inner city or outer suburb? Town or country?

A house or unit? Each has its own advantages. Houses have a higher land content, so are usually more expensive to purchase. Rates, services, repairs and maintenance cost more. Units are cheaper, unless you buy a luxury unit with gyms, pools and lifts. All are expensive to run and your levies are high. If you buy a unit, you must budget for the strata levy but your council, water and maintenance will usually be much lower than for a house. The capital gain potential is greater on a house, but a unit is a good starting point, so always try for the best position in the block. You can change the kitchen but not the position!

Buy new if you are in full-time work or dislike organising renovations. If you have to employ someone it immediately eats into your capital. However, if you are a handy person, doing up a property is a sure way of making money. Try learning how to do simple repairs yourself. Check that a job is well done and to be aware of any overcharging or shoddy work. Consult a licensed builder if things are not up to scratch. Timber properties need to be painted every few years. Best to avoid these unless you enjoy painting!

Inner city, outer suburbs or country? Position will depend largely on the finance available. Check the availability of off-street parking. In the inner city, this can add greatly to the rent return and resale value. The proximity of schools, shops, transport and open space all have a bearing on rental return and the capital growth. A water frontage or a view is a sure way to make millions, but you may need millions to buy it!

Buying another property near your home makes for easier repairs and maintenance, and you can keep an eye on the value and the growth potential of the district. Everybody has their own ideas about where to buy and what the next growth area will be. Our theory has always been to buy where we could happily live ourselves, and so far this has proved to be a sensible and profitable yardstick.

The inner city, suburbs or large provincial areas are all investment possibilities if you have done your research thoroughly. A small country town or lovely cottage may offer what looks like a great bargain but finding a tenant can take time. You are dependant on a small population that may rely on seasonal workers.

The management of your property is a two-edged sword. You can manage it yourself and cope with the problems, large and small, or you can pay an agent a small percentage of the rent (try to negotiate the amount) to run it for you. Both the tenants and the landlords have rights, administered by the Office of Fair Trading in your state. If you choose to manage it yourself, you need to know these rights and how to draw up a lease and set the bond, (usually four weeks rent), which has to be lodged with a rental bond authority. The Real Estate Institute (REI) in each state has a standard lease form. The rent can be paid directly into your bank either by the tenant or by your agent.

If you engage an agent to manage your property, give them an upper limit on the amount they can spend on running repairs without your approval. This keeps the tenant happy as simple repairs can be attended to quickly.

We are often asked if a holiday home is a good investment. Our experiences show that the peak rental period usually occurs at the time that you would like to be there, and that the off season rent barely covers the expenses. A holiday home is not really an investment — it's a luxury. Remember that you are undertaking the running of two houses — two lots of washing, two fridges to fill and two lots of cleaning. Also, you may feel committed to the same area each holiday. We opt for a motel — someone else does all the work!

> **Elizabeth** Last year we owned a townhouse and a small farm and then we purchased a beach house for the family's use. I found bookings became a problem, on top of which I had seven refrigerators — some for food and others for drinks (grandchildren have an insatiable thirst) — to keep filled and clean! The beach house didn't last long.

There are tax advantages to be noted in your equation when considering a property investment, but we advise not to buy just for the tax deductions. This is a good time to consider using an accountant, as all expenses of running the property, interest, insurance, levies, rates, repairs and maintenance and depreciation can be claimed in the earning of a taxable income.

If the costs of running the investment property exceed the income, the ability to charge this as a tax deduction against your gross income will depend on whether the Tax Office views the property as a viable future income-earning investment.

Be aware that replacing a structural item, such as a timber garage with a brick one, is a capital improvement and is added to the property's cost base for capital gains tax. It is not deductible from rental income.

You can also take out a 'loss of income' insurance which is tax deductible. Negative gearing is always associated with the buying of real estate but it can be applied to any investment. When you pay more interest than the investment is returning, this shortfall becomes a negative-geared investment.

Depreciation is the term used for 'writing off' income-producing assets through wear and tear such as stove, refrigerator, cupboards, carpets, curtains, light fittings. All can be written off over a period of years at a promulgated rate and some items can be written off entirely in the first tax year. The Australian Tax Office produces an excellent book explaining all the ins and outs.

Land tax is an annual tax not levied in all states. It is payable on investment properties and based on the Valuer-General's assessed land value, which represents the unimproved capital value (UCV) of the land only. Generally, this value is calculated for rating purposes only and does not reflect the market value. If you have doubts about your liability for land tax, consult your accountant or lawyer.

Keeping track of the income and expenses related to your investment properties is a necessary evil. Before you purchase the first property, set up a cashbook. Record the date, purchase price and all expenses relating to the property from the purchase to the first rental cheque and then all ongoing expenses and income thereafter. You will need all this for income tax purposes and, if you sell, for capital gains tax.

On completion of the purchase your lawyer/conveyancer will give you a complete rundown of all costs. The real estate agent will supply an account of the disposal of your deposit and any interest earned by it. File these statements safely, they are proof of income and expenditure.

THE COSTS OF OWNING PROPERTY

Retaining the value of your property means keeping it up to scratch. Whether it is your home or an investment, it always costs something! Apart from the mortgage, there are water or council rates to be paid, strata levies due or that leaking tap to be fixed. The outgoings are with us all the time but you can reduce some of the simple jobs with a basic tool kit and common sense. Every time a tradesman calls, that foot in the door costs!

Repairs and maintenance are ongoing expenses that must be included in the budget. When doing major work, get at least three quotes and bear in mind that the cheapest is not always the best.

Experience, reputation, co-operation and honesty are worth paying extra for. Make sure they carry their own insurance and are licensed.

We find it much better to get a quote for the complete job rather than an hourly rate. This discourages excessive talking on their mobile and long coffee breaks.

Any structural alterations or additions usually need local council approval. Without it you may be required by law to demolish them or find that a sale is difficult. Your council will give you help on this. A heritage house is a sure money-chewer, but can retain or even dramatically increase in value over a short period. Local councils and heritage groups have strict control over the outside colour and any alterations you may want to make.

The council and the neighbours hold the future of your property improvement in their hands! Before you begin, seek advice from an expert — a building consultant, architect, draftsman or lawyer. Meet with council staff to make sure you understand all the rules and regulations. Show your neighbours the plans and ask if they have any problems because it is easier to alter plans than a building. Settle all this before signing a contract with the builder.

Each state has a housing industry association and a builders' advisory service which offer advice and information on all aspects of renovation and building. Consult them before you begin — it could save you a lot of trouble.

SELLING REAL ESTATE

Before you sell, estimate the costs that could eat into any profits you are counting on. It takes time to sell — on average, about three months. Your tenants might move out because of the uncertainty or to avoid people tramping through their home. This means loss of rent until the sale is completed. Capital gains tax is payable on the profit you make on the sale. If you sell before owning a property for less than 12 months, tax is on the whole gain — you forego the concession of halving the gain before tax is assessed. Records are vital. All capital improvement expenses relating to the property must be kept from day one because these increase the cost of the property and this reduces the CGT.

Other costs include advertising and agent's commission. Try negotiating a lower rate before you sign anything. The legal fees are lower when you sell but they vary, depending on the type of property and from state to state. If the property has a mortgage then you have to factor in the cost of the release and the payout. Tidy it up before you put it on the market, but don't go overboard. Just have it looking at its best, the new owner may not like your taste.

A contract of sale is required by most states. It should be drawn up by your lawyer or conveyancer and list all inclusions and exclusions or anything unusual about your property. Decide on the method of sale that suits you — private, through an agent or at auction. Don't be rushed into an auction because they are more costly to you and they can be disappointing. However, if several buyers really want your property, then the price can 'run'.

Discuss with the agent the price you will accept, the commission and all other costs relating to the sale before they start showing people through. Arrange inspection times for when your property looks its best and brightest — season, sun and peak hour traffic noise all have an influence on buyers. Keep the place tidy with curtains open, flowers, uncluttered surfaces and so on to make it attractive to that potential buyer.

There is always a price at which a property will sell. If you don't find a buyer then you may have to wait until the market catches up with your expectations. Renting it on a short-term lease while you wait is not a bad idea, and allows time for a new set of buyers to enter the market.

Bits & Bytes
We think property investment is an essential part of every portfolio. Don't stop at one like the second and third child, it becomes less frightening and gets easier with more experience.

9. YOUR OWN BUSINESS

• • •

> I like work: it fascinates me. I can sit and look at it for hours. I love to keep it by me: the idea of getting rid of it nearly breaks my heart.
> Jerome K. Jerome

More than a quarter of a million women own a small business in Australia, making us a growing force in this world —and their business survival rate is good. Women are breaking into the service, construction and transport industries and using their initiative to develop new ideas. Now, when a woman comes up with a bright idea and develops it to the point where she needs to raise finance, money providers are willing to listen and advise.

Setting up your own business may not be your first choice but circumstances often force the issue. We now have the 'outsource' syndrome, or there are young children needing care, or maybe a health problem. On the plus side, it's amazing how often another door opens — look for it — you could end up becoming an entrepreneur. Being your own boss is always an attractive option and working from home has its advantages.

DOWNSIZED? DON'T PANIC!

Downsized, redundant, retrenched, retired early — in a word, sacked. Don't panic, it is a part of a modern working life and has led to many exciting new career changes. Certainly you are not alone. The initial shock and the worry over loss of regular cash flow can overwhelm us and muddy our thinking. You might be downsized in the Growth Years when many women plan to pick up the careers put aside because of family commitments.

Retrenchment is a blow — don't let it affect your confidence.

What do you do? Where do you start? Will your money hold out? These and other questions will go round in your head day and night. If you receive a redundancy package don't blow it! This money is important and how you handle it and make it work requires a lot of thought, research and advice.

Whether or not your ex-employer offers you a position as an 'outsourcer' or consultant, it's vital that you don't spend that pay-out before seeking advice, as there are tax implications. You may be able to pay something off that mortgage, go further into the investment world or use it to set up a small business. The options that open up will be both exciting and challenging. Work out exactly what you want to do. Now you have a chance to make money for yourself.

OUTSOURCING

Outsourcing is happening in many fields and it makes a lot of sense, both for the employer and for the outsourcer. You certainly gain more freedom and, unlike setting up your own business, have fewer up-front expenses and lower on-going costs. If you do not have the security of a contract, you have to cope with an unpredictable cash flow until you have established a wide customer base.

Being a consultant may not be what you want but if your former employer offers it, take it. It will give you breathing space while you establish yourself. Be prepared to adjust to doing without an employer's resources — a nice office, back-up help, phone, fax and stationery and stamps.

The home office

Working from a home office can be ideal for many women, especially those who care for young children or an elderly parent. You probably spent a large part of the working day coping with traffic and delivering kids to various care centres or school. By the time you got to the office, you were exhausted and angry. Goodbye to all that! The technological revolution links your home to the whole world. Your wardrobe and travel are reduced, there are no more child care fees, you are there if sickness strikes.

The flip side includes trying to have a business conversation while children erupt into chaos in the next room and friends and neighbours drop in for a chat because you're at home. You have to handle these situations with great tact or you'll end up losing the 'people' contact we all need.

Men, too, are now discovering the advantages of this lifestyle as more and more of them are retrenched. The Australian Bureau of Statistics reports that nearly half the men running a home office are over 50 while most of the women operating from home are under 50. In fact, most women working this way are between the ages of 30–49, which is when children dominate their lives.

Before you start, designate the space that is yours and yours alone. Sharing with a partner or child can cause conflict which takes time and energy to resolve. Hiring a specialist who will come to your home and design a small, workable office (even under the stairs) could pay off in terms of efficiency. Their cost is low compared to buying separate computer stands, desks, bookcases and filing cabinets. A tax deduction can be claimed for running the home office, such as a percentage of any mortgage repayments, electricity, telephone, water and council rates.

The purchase price of your computer is just the tip of the iceberg. There is the cost of installation, software programs and stationery. You might consider leasing equipment as an option as this allows you to keep your working capital intact. Using it for a set time at a set cost can make budgeting easier. Many companies also offer the option to purchase the equipment at the residual value when the lease finishes. The bonus is that lease payments are usually fully tax deductible.

Setting up a home office can affect the capital gains tax-free status of your home, whether you are self-employed or an employee who telecommutes. When you sell your home, the Taxation Office assesses the space that was used as a home office where you

produced an assessable income, and levies CGT accordingly. The Tax Office defines a home office as:
- set aside exclusively as a place of business
- clearly identified as a place of business
- not readily suitable or adaptable for private or domestic purpose.

SETTING UP A BUSINESS

You've got a great idea and the skills to carry it through. Take the bull by the horns, but be certain that you have the necessary motivation and can do without the daily chatter by the coffee machine. Be honest and self-critical, and assess the benefits and risks as realistically as possible.

If you're starting from scratch, buying an established business or a franchise, you need to have the knowledge and experience to compete with the opposition. Your day is now 25 hours, holidays are a thing of the past and sick leave — forget it! You are now the boss and the amount you earn is entirely in your hands.

Many ventures fail within the first two to three years, mainly due to a lack of financial planning and management skills. Whether or not your business involves getting extra finance, seek advice from your accountant or lawyer. If you are buying into a venture, it is essential to ask the vendor for copies of all paperwork including invoices, cash flows and stockholdings. Show them to your advisers and ask for a report.

Sudden acceptance of your product can tempt you to expand too quickly and this can be your downfall. When the first flush of custom slows down to a steady rate you can find yourself overstocked, overstaffed and no cash flow.

Free media exposure is one of the best ways to promote yourself and your business. The local newspapers are always on the lookout for interesting copy and exposure in these may lead to wider coverage. Check them out.

Starting from scratch

Before you attempt to set up a business, do your research:
- Is there sufficient demand for your product or service?
- How many others are selling the same products or services?
- What is the advantage of your product?
- Why hasn't someone thought of this before?
- Do you have enough money to start and exist?

Deciding whether to work from home, rent premises or buy a property all come into the equation. Meeting legal requirements, obtaining permits, council approval and licences will take time and money. Before committing yourself, seek advice from your accountant, solicitor and the relevant trade and professional associations. The more research you do before you take the plunge the more likely you are to succeed. All states have a department to advise small business, and it is well worth an appointment with a list of queries you need answered.

Buying a business

Before committing yourself, ask the following:
- Why is the business for sale?
- How long has it been profitable? (The books will show this story.)
- How much stock are you buying and what is its value?
- Is the location likely to lose its appeal? (e.g. is there a new freeway planned?)
- Who is the competition?
- Who are your neighbours?

One of the best ways to learn about a business is to work in it. You soon find out the pitfalls and you may also see gaps that can be exploited. If you can arrange part-time work in the business you are considering buying, even better.

The selling price will include goodwill, an intangible asset. If there is stock, arrange your own stocktake. Talk to people in the street, gather as much information as possible. Become a customer in neighbouring shops and look at the shopping flow.

Kerry Three years ago I decided to start my own hairdressing business, after having worked in a salon for some years. I had saved well and bought a half-share in a unit which my accountant advised me to sell, rather than apply for a loan from the bank. He said that as a young single woman I would be hard- pressed to get a loan for a first business. I took his advice and sold this investment. Deciding location was a first priority, I found a hairdressing business for sale that was close to many of my clients and to home. A big plus was that I would be the only hairdresser in the vicinity.

My accountant has been one of my greatest assets. He set up my books which I keep up to date, and he reconciles my bank statements. Every few months he checks them over, and does my tax returns. A major problem arose when the bank lost all the papers for setting up the business accounts. Another shock came with the unexpected amount I have to pay on credit card transactions (they are much higher for small business operators). Public risk, worker's compensation, superannuation and equipment insurance are an annual slug. At the end of the first year the Tax Office did an audit and I found it helpful, certainly not a threat. My advice is: if the tax people call, don't panic, they will make it easy.

Buying a franchise

This involves a capital outlay, often a large one. It is a business with a structured system that is replicated in various sites. It follows a set formula and has a product with a track record. (It is wise to check this). You must abide by the established rules set out in your franchise agreement. Ask your solicitor to check this before you sign. The franchisor is obligated to provide services and training, and to give you exclusive rights in your territory, all of which is covered by your agreement.

A franchise does not leave you totally alone — nor do you have total independence. You pay part of your income to the franchisor in return for backup from experienced people with advertising and marketing support. Before entering a franchise agreement check these points:

- Make sure you have exclusive territory and that you receive compensation if this is breached.
- Make sure there are adequate training programs for you and your employees.
- Check all prices of goods supplied.

The franchise world is complicated. Ask an established franchisee whether the franchisor provides the entire backup and is approachable.

USEFUL TERMS

The terms, *limited* companies (Ltd), *proprietary* companies (Pty) and *no liability* companies (NL), have been given many definitions. We have interpreted them as follows.

Limited companies Commercial public companies incorporated under the companies act with limited liability. The main factor is that shareholders are liable only for the amount of capital they have invested in the business. Such companies are required to add the word '*limited*' or its abbreviation, Ltd, to their title.

Proprietary companies Private companies which must restrict the number of shareholders to 50. They are not permitted to offer their shares to or obtain funds from the public. These companies must add the words '*proprietary limited*' or Pty Ltd to the end of their title.

No liability companies Public companies, usually mining, whose shareholders cannot be sued for any unpaid portion of their share holding. However, a shareholder's failure to meet a 'call' by the company to fully pay those shares means their shares can be forfeited. These companies must add the words *'no liability'* or NL to the end of their title.

THE COSTS OF SETTING UP A BUSINESS

Whether you plan to operate as a sole trader, a partnership, a company or a trust, some sort of structure must be set in place. They all have advantages and disadvantages, so seek advice as to what will suit your particular circumstances, taking into account things like tax, superannuation, insurance and liability. Before you can open your doors to begin trading you must register the name of your business with the relevant authority in your state and consult the tax office. A legal eagle is essential too.

Insurance and tax are necessary evils. Business expense insurance is worth considering because it will cover the normal day to day running expenses if you are unable to work due to injury or sickness. Consult an insurance broker about public risk and general insurance (they can be combined into one policy), and about worker's compensation and super which have become very complicated. Your insurance broker will also talk about disability and trauma insurances. They can be expensive and selective in their coverage. Look at the entitlement clauses and check the fine print thoroughly.

> **Anne** In 1983 when I developed rheumatoid arthritis, the sickness and accident insurance policy I held had a clause in the fine print which released the company from paying any benefits if the policyholder was able to continue to do even a small amount of work. As I was able to continue some work as a freelance editor from my bed, I was unable to claim any benefits.

The Government has decreed that all employers must contribute to a superannuation scheme for each worker. The rules are constantly changing — since its inception in the early 1980s, the scheme has been altered more than 2,000 times. You need an expert in super to set a fund in place for yourself and when you begin employing staff.

Tax is also a complicated issue when you start your own business and keeping accurate books is essential for all forms of taxation. BAS (Business Activity Statement) covers the GST (goods and services tax). PAYG (pay-as-you-go) tax applies if you employ anyone — you are responsible for deducting tax from their paypacket and remitting it to the Tax Office on a regular basis. Casual or freelance workers (paid by the job or hour) take care of their own tax commitments. Part-time workers have entitlements to some benefits in ratio to the hours they work.

If you have more than ten people on your payroll, you have other levies to consider, such as the Training Guarantee Levy (for staff education). In addition, records must be kept for fringe benefits tax (FBT), stock and stock writeoffs, car expenses, capital expenditure on equipment and petty cash. A cashbook is necessary for everyday items such as stationery, stamps, telephones and electricity. Consult your accountant on all aspects of tax and how to start and run your records.

Staff will be needed as your business grows. As the boss, be wary of becoming bosom friends with your staff, and we advise against sharing your leisure time or personal confidences. By all means, be friendly but it is essential that you never let that final barrier be crossed, you may live to regret taking this further.

You have to learn how to hire and fire and keep your eyes open for signs of disruption or any undermining tactics. If a staff member starts ignoring directives, being uncooperative, using delay tactics or spending too much time on tea or loo breaks, you will need to address the problem promptly. This is a difficult area as legislation is in place to prevent unfair dismissals.

Many people think they have a book in their head and that it might be a bestseller. Anne, a retired publisher, advises trying your hand at it. Keep in mind, though, that the chances of the bestseller are about one in 10,000! Of the 3,000 unsolicited manuscripts that crossed Anne's desk each year, she would publish only one, if that.

Direct selling is often promoted as a quick dollar earner and while some people have made a lot, far more have gone broke. It is hard work and often requires a large outlay for stock and transport.

Some state government organisations specialise in helping small businesses, and others will help if you crack the overseas market with your product. A private enterprise may be willing to listen and assist a small operation on its way. There are numerous magazines and books on running a small business.

EDUCATION AND TRAINING

Education is essential in today's world. A tertiary qualification multiplies your professional options. However, if you left school at 15, like we did, survival depends on being a quick learner and on knowing which opportunity to seize and which to let pass by.

Any kind of education or training costs, but it is more than worth the work, heartache and expense. At long last it has become the norm for women to succeed — and excel — in all professional fields.

At the start of a working life many newly qualified graduates have to be content with a position that does not use the skills they've acquired. As experience and maturity grow, the financial return and mental stimulation increase quickly and for those with qualifications employment choices are much wider.

The universities abound with mature-age students, and most of them are women starting or completing degrees. A good percentage of them did not have the finance necessary to matriculate, let alone for a tertiary education when they were young. Secretarial work, school teaching or nursing were the only choices for most of us who are now over 60. It is now possible to graduate in any field you like if you have the required qualifications or experience. Sometimes an interview will get you in but you will need to be able to find the fees. Nowadays, it is not unheard of for three female generations of a single family to end up in the same class!

Many educational institutions repeat courses throughout the year and schedule them at all hours of the day and night. You can attend a short course through an evening college covering the basics of running a small business, or you may prefer to study full-time and gain a degree in business studies from a tertiary institution. If you can't leave home there's always open learning on television.

10. TAXING MATTERS

• • •

> But in this world nothing can be said to be certain,
> except death and taxes.
> *Benjamin Franklin*

Tax has many different meanings. Besides the compulsory financial contribution that looms largest in our minds, there are those aspects of life that tax our intellect and attention, such as powers of attorney, wills, joint accounts, and other money matters.

Bits & Bytes

Tax is not new! They were collecting it in Mesopotamia and Egypt in ancient times as customs duty on goods imported from other countries. The first record of income tax in Britain is dated 1799, when the Prime Minister William Pitt levied a 10 per cent tax to help pay for the Napoleonic Wars.

TAXATION

One of the most unpopular professions down through the ages has been that of the 'tax gatherer'. They are still with us and we still have to pay taxes. As long as we expect the leaders of our communities to organise and supply services, we have to pay for them. All levels of government — federal, state and local — levy taxes in the following forms:

Goods and Services Tax (GST) A tax on consumption, at present set at a flat 10 per cent on goods and services with few exceptions.

Income tax Paid by individuals and levied annually on a progressive scale: the more you earn, the more you pay.

Pay as you go (PAYG) Brings instalments of income tax and other liabilities together in one system. Whether you pay annually or quarterly depends on your taxable income.

Company tax Paid on gross profits, before the distribution of dividends at a rate set by the Federal Government budget. All companies pay the same rate of tax.

Capital gains tax Levied on profits made on the sale of goods that have been purchased with a view to gain.

Excise duty Levied on goods such as tobacco and alcohol paid by the consumer.

Customs duty Paid on imported goods. When you travel overseas you can buy duty-free goods but you must take them with you as part of your luggage. There is a strict limit to what you can bring back into Australia.

Rates Apply to water, council, rubbish disposal and are a form of local government taxes on property owners.

Land tax A state tax based on the land content only of investment properties, and on homes over a promulgated value. This tax is not levied by all states.

GOODS AND SERVICES TAX (GST)

GST was introduced in Australia in July 2000, as part of a broad-based consumption tax package. Its aim is to reduce the general rate of income tax and to remove many state taxes as the states are the main recipients of this revenue. GST is levied at a set rate, at present 10 per cent, on almost all the goods and services that we require.

Taxpayers are divided into three main groups.

1. Those who provide goods or services and are registered with the ATO. These are mainly companies and include any small business whether it employs staff or is a sole trader. An Australian Business Number (ABN) is issued as the identifying number for all dealings with government.

    A GST number is also issued to enterprises who on-sell, to register them as required to submit a business activity statement (BAS). The BAS records the amount of GST a trader has paid and collected while providing goods or services. One amount can be offset against the other, ensuring that GST is paid only once on each transaction. This tax is paid to the ATO quarterly or yearly, depending on turnover.
2. Those who require only an ABN. This covers all activities which do not involve reselling either goods or services. For example, if a writer does not have an ABN, their publisher is unable to claim any GST incurred by the producing and selling of the book.
3. Those who do not have to get involved in providing or selling goods or services. This group simply submits a tax return each year, provided their income is over $6,000 per year.

INCOME TAX

Income tax is the major form of taxation that directly affects us all. Careful planning can help take advantage of the concessions allowed. Well-kept books, receipts filed in a logical way and notes on any unusual transactions are all a great help at tax time. If you do your own tax read the Tax Pack thoroughly before you start. It gives easy to follow step-by-step instructions and details all your rights.

The Tax Pack lists legitimate deductions that PAYG earners can subtract from their income before tax is assessed. Business and investment deductions are more complicated and you may need Tax Office advice. As your investments grow, more schedules are required. A tax agent or accountant will save you money and frustration. Remember, their fees are tax-deductible.

Superannuation with its income tax benefits, pay-ins, pay-outs and after-death aspects, needs careful treatment. The rules are being changed all the time and few of us have enough knowledge to negotiate this minefield, so seek expert advice..

PAYG

This is a scheme that replaces provisional tax. The ATO will inform you if you are liable for this tax and will send you an assessment of the amount payable and the date due — quarterly or annually, depending on your assessed income for the next tax year. An Instalment Activity Statement is the form on which you report your tax obligations, and the percentage payable is worked out for you by the ATO. PAYG is an integrated system for reporting and paying tax on income earned through business and investment.

If you are an employee only, with no other income such as investments, rental properties or partnerships, then PAYG will not affect you. However, your employer must still deduct Pay As You Earn (PAYE) from your wages and provide you with a certificate, stating the amount already paid to the Tax Office, at the end of the financial year.

Since there are many more records that PAYG taxpayers must keep, we strongly recommend consulting a bookkeeper or accountant. Your time is money and if you can't earn more than you pay a bookkeeper, something is wrong somewhere!

An honest mistake

Tax legislation is complex and it is very easy to make an inadvertent mistake if doing your own tax return. The ATO is not an ogre, and if it considers that you have taken 'reasonable care' it will probably give you the benefit of the doubt and help you sort it out without a fine. However, if they do not think your error is reasonable, you may face a stiff penalty. Never be afraid to ask the ATO for help. We have often sought their advice and have had our problem solved without hassles.

Tax audit
The words scare everyone. If you are randomly selected for an audit, you are required to present complete records (on disc or paper) of all financial transactions, including bank statements. Try to have your accountant present. If you are running your own business, keep up-to-date with everything from BAS to stock records — it makes the process easier. An audit requires records covering the last five years for a personal return, and records covering the last seven years for a business return.

To avoid any misunderstanding between you and the auditors, do not answer any questions you do not understand. A tax audit costs time and money. The best way to reduce these costs is to be properly prepared so that the audit can be completed as quickly as possible.

The Tax Office will, of course, become curious if your lifestyle is grander than your taxable income would suggest.

Be careful of so-called 'tax breaks' that seem to run in fashions. One year it is ostrich farms and the next it's the latest dot.com venture. These rarely return you anything like the money you put in.

CAPITAL GAINS TAX
Capital gains tax is simply a tax on any capital gain made on an asset. The Australian Tax Office (ATO) considers that you have acquired an asset whether you buy it, inherit it, construct it or receive it as a gift. An asset is deemed to have been disposed of when you sell it, give it away or you lose or destroy it.

Capital gains tax is a tax on the difference between the purchase price and the sale price of an asset — be it real estate, shares, artwork, collectables or any item with resale possibilities. If you sell an asset acquired after 20 September 1985 and before 21 September 1999 you have two choices for assessing the tax obligation: one is based on indexing and the second is based on halving the realised nominal gain. This sounds complicated, but the Tax Office will help you readily, at no cost.

The indexed cost base is tied to the consumer price index (CPI) for each quarter from the purchase date to the sale date. The formula used for indexing is complex, requiring a great deal of mathematics to work out each quarter's index formula. The Tax Office has all the CPI figures you need.

The new nominal gain method is much simpler. No CPI is involved, just the cost base (the price paid plus the costs of buying) and the sale price (the price received less the costs of selling). Subtract one from the other to assess whether you have a capital gain, 50 per cent of which is added to your assessable income. A loss can be offset against capital gains.

For all purchases made after 21 September 1999 use only the nominal gain method to assess the CGT. Once you have grasped the principle it is just another tax. Selling dead heads (the ones not living up to your expectations) in the same tax year that you make a 'killing' can help reduce your overall tax.

It is essential to keep full records of all expenditures incurred by any asset that attracts CGT, not just for your own sake when you dispose of them but also for anyone who will inherit from you. Complete records of expenditure also protect you against paying more tax than necessary.

The records you need to keep include:
- documents showing date and cost of purchase;
- documents showing date of sale and amount received;
- market valuation of an inheritance at date of receipt.

Some expenses can be laid against the cost of an asset, so keep all documentation of:
- legal fees for purchase and sale;
- agent's commission, brokerage fees;

- stamp duty (not charged in all states);
- costs of all improvements.

The ATO produces an excellent book *Guide to Capital Gains Tax* which is updated as required, and is free. It has sample recording pages and its explanations are simple. They print many other guides that cover all tax-related matters, well worth getting.

The most important thing to remember about CGT is to keep as many details of assets as possible. Even a letter sent to you with a gift can help to establish date of receipt and ownership. You can be fined if you do not keep proper records, so be sure rather than sorry — but you may need to install an attic to store it all, as we have done!

If you own your own home and bought it after 20 September 1985, and you have run your business from home, or rented part of it, you may be liable for CGT on that portion of the house used for the business or rented. On real estate purchased for investment, the capital gains clock starts ticking from the day you sign the contract, not when you pay for it.

If you inherit an asset you must record the valuation at the date of its previous owner's death and keep records of any costs of administering the estate. This is the amount the asset is deemed to have cost you and on which CGT will be levied if you sell. If you inherit shares, keep a copy of the financial pages of the newspaper published on the day of death (showing the date) to give you a record of the share prices on that day.

All assets from divorce or separation are also affected by the 20 September 1985 ruling. CGT does not apply to the future sale of any joint assets acquired before then, if the acquisition is the result of a court order. If they are acquired after that date you should ask for details of all costs. Remember that when assets are transferred between spouses, no CGT will be imposed on the transfer — but by the same token, no loss is granted if in the future you dispose of the asset. It is a good idea to clarify all this with your solicitor and the ATO before final settlement.

POWER OF ATTORNEY

The power of attorney is not just something for the old and infirm. It is a legal document, which should be drawn up by a solicitor, that gives to another person or persons the right to act on your behalf in all matters.

There are two types of power of attorney.

A general power of attorney can be given a set expiry date or purpose. If you die before that date or event, it terminates.

The enduring power of attorney has no time limit, so if you end up in a coma or develop Alzheimer's disease, the person you have appointed will continue to run your affairs until your death. You can appoint more than one person to act for you. It must be signed while you are considered fully responsible for your decision.

The document needs to be registered with the Register General of Deeds or the Land Titles Office. When a power of attorney is activated, the person you appoint takes over for you. If you are in business, own property or investments, or if you travel, appoint someone to act on your behalf if you are rushed to hospital, or even if you are simply travelling somewhere remote. Otherwise, if the stock market crashes — you could come home to no income.

When you give someone your power of attorney you are giving them absolute control to act for you. Choose someone you trust implicitly and discuss it with them fully. They are undertaking a tremendous responsibility, and one which might involve a lot of work. Powers of attorney should not to be given out lightly, or you could find your assets stripped and no redress available.

You can give the document to them if you are making an extended trip, but take this important document back on your return until you need to call on their help again. To cancel a registered power of attorney, notify in writing all parties, including the Register General of Deeds. Always lodge a copy with your solicitor so he or she knows who is handling your affairs.

> **Anne** My mother left me her enduring power of attorney when she went overseas for an extended trip

to visit family. Several months after her return she was diagnosed as suffering from Alzheimer's disease. I was able to use this power of attorney to manage her finances, sell the real estate and use the proceeds to keep my mother in a good nursing home (she went on to live another 16 years). One tip I would recommend is that you make several certified copies of the power of attorney. This makes it much easier when you have to sell shares or real estate or move investments around as some institutions require certified copies. Some banks keep a copy on their files, which means you don't have to take the original with you every time you make a transaction.

The only things a power of attorney does not have the power to do is to change the terms of your will, give evidence in court on your behalf or enter into any transaction that could cause a conflict of interest.

MAKING A WILL

Unless you can emulate Lazarus, make a will now. Age has nothing to do with it. The minute you have possessions and wish to control what happens to them when you die, you need a will. It is a legal and binding document, so precise terminology is important if you do not wish to leave behind heartache and headaches. Most problems can be avoided if you ask a solicitor or a trustee company to draw one up. A simple will can be made for a small fee, some as low as $100.

You need to appoint at least one executor to carry out your wishes. This can be quite a demanding and time-consuming job, so ask your executor before naming them in your will, or use a trustee company. You need more than one, but if you appoint too many executors or trustees, you will give your family a 'camel' and nothing will be done in a hurry!

All executors are entitled to a fee but friends or family usually waive this. As your wealth grows (with wise investment of your 10 per cent) and circumstances change, you need to update. You can make a codicil at any time to add or subtract from an existing will, but don't add too many as it only causes confusion. Make sure your executor knows where your current will is kept — you don't want your weeping family searching high and low.

A will needs two witnesses, who must see you sign it. Then you watch them sign and date the document. Remember, a witness cannot be a beneficiary

When you die without a valid will, you die *intestate*. Strict legal rules, which differ from state to state, determine what happens to your estate. If you leave children it can be complicated and hard for them. Think of the mess if you have a business, a partnership, dependant partner, parent or children needing care. Your entire estate is tied up until the legal eagles sort out it out, secure probate and release it.

We don't recommend using the do-it-yourself will kits available from stationers. Following professional advice from your solicitor or a trustee company is the only way to be certain that you don't leave behind a will that can be challenged through the courts by warring relatives. Make it as simple as possible — you can't foresee every eventuality but you can't rule from the grave either.

Marriage revokes any previous will. If you remarry, then die without having made a new will, your new spouse will be better off and any children from a previous marriage will be worse off. A decree absolute to dissolve a marriage revokes any appointment of your former husband as executor and any gift you may have bequeathed him.

If you leave little notes around the house, giving your favourite vase to cousin Jane, and there is a dispute, the Probate Office will decide whether these notes can be accepted as codicils to your will. They can cause considerable distress, expense and delay!

Capital gains tax can also encroach on your estate. When making your will, study the ramifications of the legislation when you divide your possessions in your will. It is essential to keep all paperwork relating to investments and your home. To avoid favouring one beneficiary over another unwittingly, ask your lawyer for an explanation of this complicated aspect of taxation.

JOINT ACCOUNTS

Be careful. Whether for business, marriage or any partnership, do not sign any paper without being fully aware of what you are signing.

Many women sign away their financial freedom and spend the rest of their life paying off a partner's mismanagement of joint capital. Banks are becoming aware of this problem and most now check that both partners know what they are signing, especially if a loan or mortgage is involved. It is safer to go one step further and ask a solicitor to explain any documents you are asked to sign. If you take out a joint loan of any description, a creditor can pursue you and even bankrupt you if payment of the debt is late or not forthcoming. You can even be forced to pay for your partner's sports car and never have the pleasure of driving it.

Operating any joint financial account has its dangers. It can be drained without your knowledge, leaving you high and dry. Check the statement of your accounts regularly for any alarming discrepancy in the balance.

Strike out any clauses in the loan agreement you don't approve of and fix a limit for any overdraft. Protect yourself and remember that the creditor, most likely a bank manager, will also protect himself or herself from any head office backlash. In any case, all agreements will be weighted in the lender's favour, not in yours.

MONEY AND PARTNERSHIP

> Never marry for money.
> You can borrow it cheaper.
> *Anon*

All too many of us set up with a partner without paying enough attention to the financial side of the relationship, and end up making some terrible mistakes. The pitfalls of combining accounts, incomes, expenditure, debts, loans and investments are great. A lot of thought and discussion is necessary before you commit yourself to these. It is a great mistake for partners in any relationship to avoid talking about money because it is unromantic.

Two incomes A common approach is to invest one partner's income while the other pays the housekeeping bills. If the relationship fails, however, you risk finding that all the investments are in one name — your partner's.

Signing mortgages Never sign anything without reading and understanding what you are being asked to sign. Have all documents checked by your own lawyer.

Cash control Never allow your partner to control the cash flow just to show your faith and love. This is not sensible. If something happens to your partner, you need to know all about the finances.

Gift or inherited money Never put any large amounts straight into joint names without discussing it fully. It could be better to put it in your name only, and may be what the giver intended.

Keep a set of books listing both salaries, all assets, insurance and superannuation. Also, list all expenses involving housekeeping, repayment of loans, investment money, general expenses and how much each of you wants as 'pocket money'. Keeping this list flexible and reviewing it regularly will save a lot of arguments and heartaches. Every woman needs money of her own, so make sure this is included in the budget.

If a relationship breaks down, and bank accounts are in your partner's name, you are not automatically entitled to money in those accounts unless you can prove your contributions. Keep records.

Knowing about family finances is not just for beginning partnerships, it is for all of us at all ages. Good records and a working knowledge of the finances will save you much anxiety if you have to cope with separation, divorce, or the death of your partner.

11. CUTTING COSTS

Creditors have better memories than debtors.
Benjamin Franklin

With your budget in front of you and your net worth assessed, see if you need to adjust your spending to put you further in front.

Check your food bills for luxuries you can manage without. Read the back of your supermarket dockets for cash-saving offers. Watch your power consumption: shorter showers are the order of the day. We are living in a 'fast' world — fast food, fast cash, mobiles, faxes, Internet — and fast is expensive. Some old-fashioned ways are cheaper — get up early, pack your lunch, or make it the night before.

Stationery from a newsagent or stationery shop is expensive. Discount and variety stores stock everything from manila folders to computer paper. Even the Post Office has special deals.

When you own a house there is always something that has to be done. Cut costs and gain satisfaction by learning to do a few simple repairs and maintenance jobs yourself — anyone can change a fuse.

Every time you turn around, someone has their hand out! If it's not the kids, it's the bank. Not opening your purse to these continuing demands is one of the hardest lessons you have to learn, yet it is the first step towards financial security. As we explain in the relevant chapter (chapters 3 and 4), huge savings can be made on your bank fees, and as for credit cards — cut them up!

COSTS OF BEING A WORKING WOMAN

Standing on your own two feet is expensive, especially for women. Until we have equal pay for equal work right across the board, we will remain behind the eight ball. Meanwhile, we have to be self-disciplined, identify the problems, and find a way around them.

Going to work

This, of course, has its own inbuilt expenses, such as clothes. A senior bank executive we know has managed to look presentable for two years in two suits! Fares, lunches and after work wind-downs all strain the budget. As we climb the corporate ladder our wardrobe must change and estimates suggest that it costs a woman on the mid-rung 30 per cent more than her male counterpart for her wardrobe, not counting make-up and hairdressing. A good quality dual-season wardrobe is a money saver, so follow the sales and the factory outlets. Stick to the classic lines, they will last for years, particularly if you have a range of accessories and can mix and match.

Delay each appointment with the hairdresser by a couple of days; at the end of the year you will be in front. Remember that many of the cheaper shampoos and face creams have the same basic ingredients as the expensive ones, so check the labels.

Home responsibilities

Once these start the short working day disappears and the logistics of living become problematic. Today's woman spends about 30 hours a week on domestic chores including shopping, while men spend half that time, much of it outdoors, gardening or pool cleaning. It is hard to find reliable domestic help. Word of mouth is the best way. Make sure your salary is sufficient to cover this expense. Remember it is coming out of your after-tax earnings. It may be viable to cut your working hours and do the chores yourself.

Childcare

This is a major cost for working mothers and suitable carers are hard to find. Even then you can spend half the daylight hours in the car delivering and collecting. If you have several children, a private 'nanny' may be cheaper. Informal childcare — relying on grandparents, friends or neighbours — is one option that many of us take. It does have its problems, but they are not insurmountable. If you are offered childcare as part of your workplace package, you are one of the lucky ones: stick to it like glue!

Working from home

No fares, no extensive wardrobe, and no extras such as office social functions. Eating at home can mean healthier and cheaper meals. Hang out the washing during coffee break — driers eat money! If you have small children, it is the happiest solution — you don't have to feel guilty about leaving them with someone else and you still have that cash flow which means financial independence. Home workers have the added joy of watching the children develop.

THE HOUSE

Your first big step is when you leave the family home and start on your own. Whether this happens in your spending years or further down the track, the freedom is fabulous — but, oh, the costs. If doing this without many possessions, the second-hand furniture stores are full of surprises, and as your tastes change you can sell these first purchases back again.

Buying your own home involves legal and government charges, removalists, goods and chattels, and repairs, cleaning, painting and so on. Most of these costs are unavoidable, but there are a few corners you can cut:

- Hire a truck and move yourself (with a few strong friends).
- Hire a steam cleaner to clean the carpet.
- Look for second-hand furniture bargains.
- Borrow furniture and household items from friends or family.
- Throw a working-bee housewarming party.

Renting also has its costs — leases and the bond — with the same removal and set-up costs.

Owning the roof over your head has ongoing expenses, and it is vital to keep any property that you own up to scratch if you want it to retain its value. DIY books are your first source of information on renovating, repairs and maintenance.

Contents insurance is a necessary expense. Even if you only own a television set, it can be a disaster if you come home and find it gone. Be sure to insure any large purchases such as a computer, valuable jewellery, art works and collectables. Building insurance is usually a condition of mortgage but you need it anyway, for your home or investment property. See if you can get a discount by combining all your insurances with one company. If you are a student or a senior, always ask for a discount.

THE CAR

Don't join the masses and go up to your eyeballs in debt for your first car. Remember the purchase price is just the beginning. Then follows third party insurance, comprehensive insurance and registration. These are not one-off costs as they repeat themselves every year whether you take the car out of the garage or not.

Your car is a depreciating asset and falls in value the minute you drive it off the showroom floor. A second-hand car also depreciates but not as quickly as a new one. If you are under 25, comprehensive insurance is loaded against you, supposedly taking into account that the young are accident-prone drivers.

Running costs reflect the way you use the car and how you drive it. Petrol, repairs and maintenance can be kept under control if you remember this is an expensive piece of machinery which chews petrol, particularly if you are a lead-foot. The tyres wear out every time you brake, and your car needs regular servicing. An oil change is cheaper than a new engine and regular cleaning removes the duco-destroying road dirt — use a car washing liquid that leaves a thin protective layer of wax.

Speed not only kills, it also costs. Driving at 100 km/h uses 25 per cent more petrol than it does at 90 km/h. Roof racks spoil the aerodynamics, (the car does not slip through the air as easily, so it uses more petrol), so remove them when you don't need them.

Try to resist buying an exotic model — a popular make of car will get you from A to B just as well and will cost far less. Shop around if you need finance before you visit the sales rooms. Don't buy 'more car' than you need — it will be dearer to keep on the road and harder to park.

Leasing your car makes tax sense if you are in business and need a car to earn income. There are various ways of leasing but contracts can be complicated and tie you into large payouts at the end of the lease. Get help from your accountant or financial adviser.

You used to have one, but it's never there when you want it and yet the costs go on and on and the petrol disappears. Does this sound familiar? The 'P' plate has arrived in your house!

> **Peggy** When I set up home with my 20-something daughter and a teenage son, we could afford only one car between the three of us. After several false starts we finally worked out a 'booking' system which was fair to everyone. We kept a car diary, and when one of us wanted to use the car we had to book in the date and time — if it was still available. It worked well, there were no arguments, the diary had it all recorded, and we all respected the rules.

THE CHILDREN

You can have a Ferrari, an Italian villa and a Paris wardrobe — or you can have kids! Children do give you great joy, they also bring great responsibilities and you need careful planning to give them the best start you can. Everything to do with children costs, so adjust your budget to take this into account. Plan your portfolio so that it matures or gives large dividends when they start school, and at the beginning of high school and tertiary years.

Spending Years You have nine months to get ready — the expense of just one baby is huge. You can lessen the spending by acquiring many of the essentials second-hand, and by shopping at the discount stores that specialise in children's stuff. Borrowing from friends and family is even cheaper.

Growth Years The sleepless nights are over but the expense is getting higher. Take a long hard look at your portfolio and rationalise your wants. Adjust your investments to cater for the expensive years of education.

Freedom Years They still come back often for financial help. Keep a weather eye on your portfolio and be careful not to promise so much that the freedom you have been looking forward to has to be put on hold.

Meeting the cost of education, whether public, or private, secondary or tertiary, can be your biggest single expense apart from your house. Plan early for this one, don't let it be a last minute panic. When you are starting off, so many expenses pull at your purse strings that you put off the thought of education — it seems so far away. If you are using a financial adviser, they can set up a plan to cover these years. If you are managing your own money, budget for education in your long-term investment, when you start parenthood.

Scholarships, bursaries and grants are available at all levels of education and it is essential to do your research early to take advantage of these opportunities. Bursaries are assessed more on financial needs than on academic ability.

Investing for your children or grandchildren is a great idea, but take care — it can create tax problems. Legally, an adult has to act on the child's behalf although the child is regarded as the owner of the assets and is taxed at a special rate. The Tax Office will advise you about this.

Starting children on the investment route early can boost their desire to save. When they understand how and why their investment can grow they begin to learn the complexities of the financial world.

Full health insurance is vital when you have dependants. Some funds offer excellent family packages, so research them all. Others give you extra protection for injuries at school or at sport. Insurance policies to protect your income, mortgage payments, house and contents and a life policy on top of your super are highly recommended. You can arrange a direct payment from your bank account at whatever interval suits your budget, and this may earn you a discount.

SOME MORE COST-CUTTING IDEAS

> Costly thy habit as thy purse can buy.
> Shakespeare:
> Hamlet Act 1 siii

Bulk buying is ideal for a group if you are all prepared to take a turn. Leaving it to one or two to do it just doesn't work.

Seconds shops seem to be available for everything. We have found a marvellous outlet where we can get things from toothbrushes to plastic garden pots. The up-market china manufacturers have wonderful seconds outlets.

Warehouse outlets are now big business with most capital cities running special buses around the traps. A word of warning here — don't get carried away!

Diets, fitness centres and other weight loss programs can be very expensive. Do you really need them? Try doing some exercise yourself or motivate a friend to do it with you. It's cheaper than forking out for a gym membership, and a fast walk round the block or a swim in the local pool is just as good a way to keep fit. All you need is self-discipline. Local social sports clubs can offer you social interaction as well as exercise. Look in the local paper.

Entertainment Dinner parties at home are cheaper than eating out and you can hear yourself talk. Yes, it's more work but why not plan a week of entertaining and do the shopping, preparation and the basic cooking in one day. It cuts the time and expense if you can stretch the same menu over several nights.

School holidays Many local councils and sports associations offer free holiday activities, some with all-day and sleepover happenings. Libraries and National Parks also offer entertainment. There are useful books on free and low cost entertainment, venues and so on. Grandparents are a bonus during school holidays!

12. BUYING ALONE

• • •

> Speak softly and carry a big stick.
> *Theodore Roosevelt*

A woman trying to buy a car, a boat, a motorbike or a plane on her own will find that in these domains most of the sales staff are male. Before you start, decide exactly what you want and how much you have to spend, and read and compare the specifications of them all. Don't be bluffed or intimidated — you can't afford to change brands or models in a hurry.

BUYING A CAR

The motor trade has been slow to take the lone female buyer seriously, but it is starting to realise that women are the biggest growth area in the car industry and are influencing both the design and marketing of new models. We have the cash and we are spending! Women are learning to talk the torque and are now the registered owners of at least 40 per cent of all vehicles on the road.

Buying a new car

This can be intimidating, but remember that you are the one with the money. Insist on a test drive without the salesperson continuing their spiel. Shop around: all prices are negotiable especially when you are trading in or paying cash. If you are borrowing to purchase, consider paying the registration, third party insurance and comprehensive insurance as a separate item so that you don't pay interest on these, as they are an annual cost. Try for a 'drive away' or an 'on road' price that will include stamp duty, delivery charge, registration and third party insurance.

Buying a second-hand car

This needs careful thought. You can buy at auction, through a dealer or privately. Arrange for a thorough inspection of the vehicle by a reputable mechanic — try the motoring organisations in your state. Auction is generally a cheaper way to buy but you may not be able to test drive and assessing the condition of the car is difficult. There are regulations which give you some protection but it is a buyer-beware market and auctions generate excitement — don't get carried away. Keep in mind the extra costs, such as transfer fees, stamp duty, insurance and third party insurance.

Buying from a dealer means negotiating. You will pay more than at auction but you may get a limited warranty if the car is less than 10 years old, and you can trade in your old model. You can arrange your own finances. You don't have to take the package or insurance offered by the dealer. It is usually better to stay with your own insurance company.

Buying privately, either through the press or at a car market is for the experienced. You need a careful assessment of the car. It could be mechanically OK but an engine is no use without a body fit for the roads. Before paying any money, contact the Register of Motor Vehicles to check that the car you want carries no outstanding debt that could become your problem. If it is stolen, you will have no security, it will simply be returned to the original owner. Take the vehicle identification number or chassis number and the engine number, which are engraved on a plate usually fixed to the bulkhead between the engine and passenger compartment.

> **Grace** As joint owners of a small business, my husband and I decided it was time I bought a new car. I knew exactly what I wanted, the colour and the price we could afford. My husband phoned the local agent to make a time for me to call and vaguely discussed the price. When I arrived for my test drive the salesman made the assumption that the deal was finalised, that 'the wife' was just going to have a spin around the

block and that would be it. I asked about colours and was told I had no choice. Then I asked a few technical questions which did not impress the salesman. He was even less impressed when I started to negotiate the price, telling me firmly that the price had been 'arranged with my husband'. I demanded to see the sales manager, who backed his salesman, with the result that I walked out. The next day we phoned another dealer. I finally purchased my car for the price and in the colour I wanted, with a good test drive and all my questions answered.

BUYING A BOAT, MOTORBIKE OR PLANE

The boating world is mostly male even though a woman has sailed solo around the world and female crews have taken part in world class sailing races — and been winners. A boat is a bottomless pit when it comes to money. Make sure you know this specialised area thoroughly.

A motorbike represents freedom, albeit a dangerous one. If you're keen to know more, join a club and ask to be a pillion passenger so you can learn the ins and outs of this form of transport. If you enjoy the freedom, the wind in your face and the sense of speed, ask the experts where to learn to ride. Find out what type and size of bike would suit your purse and capabilities. In general, the same rules that apply to buying a car will also apply here.

Bits & Bites
On holidays, it might be worth hiring a motor scooter by the hour to save the larger expense of hiring plus the hassle of parking a car. It's fun and you see a lot more. Hiring a little plane is a marvellous way to get an overview of the area and it's not always as expensive as it you might expect.

Buying a plane will take a large part of your first million and to be a pilot means committing to a lot of learning and expense. You will need to pass navigation and theory of flight courses, and flying hours need to be 'racked' up before you have your licence and fly solo. If you can afford a plane you can always hire a pilot!

When buying any of these fun machines take into account the hidden costs of registration, taxes and insurance and don't forget mooring, garage and hangar fees.

MAINTENANCE

Many women now complete engineering and mechanical courses but not enough are there in the workshop when you need to ask questions about your car or outboard motor. List the problems and check them off before you pay the bill.

> **Sally** My car needed two new front tyres and the back tyres swapped over so I went to a tyre specialist. After this was done, I was asked if I wanted a wheel alignment as well. I was stumped (my husband hadn't mentioned this and I'm no mechanic), so I went home without it and I was back the next day! A young guy asked 'Do you want a wheel alignment or a thrust?' I was told that a thrust would line up the front and back wheels and would cost another $20. I had thought that this was what a wheel alignment did but I went for a thrust. I later checked with mechanic friends who laughed like mad and said I'd been conned. I phoned the MVRIC (Motor Vehicle Repair Industry Council) and registered my complaint, but my $20 was gone forever.

Schools are starting up to bring women up to speed in car maintenance and advanced safe driving skills. Both are worth doing so check with your motoring association.

Shopping in a hardware store

Hardware stores have become a lot more user-friendly. You can get all the information you need on the different products available for the job you need to do. Hardware stores are full of brochures on DIY, pick them all up and file for later reference.

Tradesmen in the house

Repairs to household whitegoods can be expensive. Servicemen charge a set amount to knock on your door and then for each 15 minutes on the job. Insist on a firm quote. If it is necessary for you to be home while the job is done, remember your time is money too, so get an estimate of the time involved and a firm starting date. So don't talk or offer a cup of tea until the job is done and you have paid the serviceman.

13. INSURANCE, SUPER AND PENSIONS

• • •

The most popular labour-saving device is still money.
Phyllis George

INSURANCE

Nowadays you can insure everything and anything. Unfortunately it has become necessary to do just that — insuring all the basics — your home, car, health, life and even the kids at school. There is insurance for just about anything — even your vocal chords if you are a diva — so long as you pay.

Insurance companies and their sales representatives have been working hard on their image. Since 1 January 1996, the industry has approved three codes of practice: one to cover general insurance, a second to cover life insurance and a third to ensure that the insurance advisers and sellers adhere to a code of ethics.

There are two main groups of insurance salespeople: insurance brokers and insurance agents. A broker's responsibility is to the client. They shop around for the best policy to suit the requirements of each customer, and are independent of any specific insurance company. Agents answer to the companies they represent and sell their products and services, though some represent several companies. All brokers and agents make their income by taking commission from each company they do business for. Some may charge clients a fee for their advice.

Insurance becomes a necessity the moment you own anything — a pearl, a car, a house or a tent. It is now a necessary part of our calculations when doing the budget. As with everything connected with money, research is essential and not just for the first time you take out insurance. Conditions and premiums are changing constantly so don't fall into the easy habit of just paying up every time the renewal arrives on your desk — that could be costing you money. Some companies offer discounts if all your policies are with them, others offer deals for students and seniors. The secret is to negotiate.

General insurance

General insurance covers possessions — in fact, everything except your life and your health. You can take out separate general insurance against loss or damage to your home (its contents and the building) your car, your boat and anything else you consider at risk. An 'all risks' valuables insurance policy will cover you for loss of jewellery, cameras and valuable items anywhere in Australia. Each policy will spell out what is and isn't covered. Read the fine print carefully because some words have a special meaning to insurance companies. Ask for full explanations of everything that is not clear.

> **Bits & Bytes**
>
> A niche market for general insurance coverage has opened up for dogs, cats, even valuable fish. You can cover them for just about every illness or accident they are likely to suffer — it could be cheaper than the vet's bill. Australia has the largest rate of pet ownership in the world: 31 per cent of households are estimated to have at least one pet.

In a time of increasing litigation, ensure that your policy covers you for public risk, in case the census collector falls down your steps! Your policy should also cover any domestic help. If you live in a strata complex, make sure the Owners Corporation's insurance covers voluntary workers before you even water the common garden.

Claims for theft and damage have to be substantiated, assessed by experts and reported to the police promptly — as soon as possible after the event. Otherwise it is hard to remember exactly what happened and at what time.

Life insurance

There are many life insurance policies to cover a wide range of specific needs — life, disability, sickness and trauma. When you have children or when a parent dies, life suddenly pushes responsibilities (and insurance) to the front of your mind. Talk to several insurance brokers or agents and discuss what is best for your age and financial position. Read the fine print before signing or paying anything. Also, check to see if your superannuation agreement includes life insurance coverage.

Term life insurance This provides financial protection in the event of your death. It is renewed each time you pay the annual premium and provides a safety net for those left behind. Premiums go up as you get older, but you can avoid this rise by reducing the amount of the cover at each renewal time. A business partnership should consider a policy that covers each partner to protect everyone in the case of a partner's death.

Bits and Bytes
Life insurance has replaced the old term *life assurance* which grew out of the fact that we are assured of the termination of life.

Disability insurance As the term implies, this will cover you for any sickness or accident which prevents you from carrying out your normal occupation. As mentioned earlier in Chapter 9, this type of policy is essential if you run your own business, but it is also important for employed people as sick leave entitlements are often limited. Remember to check thoroughly all details such as when they will pay and exactly what they will cover. This kind of cover demands thorough research.

Trauma insurance This has become more common over the last few years as strokes, heart attacks and cancer seem to be hitting younger and younger people. These policies do cover other diseases (specified in the insurance company's documents) and go beyond just paying for treatment. You could pay off the mortgage, for example, or any other debt, including medical expenses, thus removing some of the stress. The company will pay out a lump sum when the illness first occurs. The premiums and your risk rise with your age. Seek advice before committing yourself to one of these policies.

There is a 'cooling off' period with every policy to give you time to digest all it contains. Don't forget that fees and government charges are usually included in the premium.

Health insurance

Private health insurance — should you or shouldn't you? Anne had been fully covered for a long time before she contracted rheumatoid arthritis many years ago while we were canoeing in the Everglades. Over the years, claim after claim has been met without problem, so in her case it has certainly paid off.

Even if you're single, young and healthy, we recommend that you assess your state of health and the risks, if any, attached to your job. Hospital covers vary greatly in the way they combine ancillary benefits. Their time and cost limits on claims also vary. If you are not a sporting person, why join the fund that offers rebates on sporting equipment but does not give you full dental cover?

Some of the funds run optical, dental and heart clinics, where the charges are minimal. Others offer travel insurance, low-cost children's accident cover and alternative health therapy cover. An ambulance ride is expensive and is not covered by Medicare. Membership of a health fund covers you for 100 per cent of this cost. If you do not take out private health insurance you can purchase ambulance only cover from some funds, though this option is not so common now.

Membership dues can be deducted direct from your salary or bank account. This may also give you a discount and saves you having to remember to pay. You have a choice of payment periods and dates, which is a help when budgeting.

In January 1999 the Federal Government offered to rebate 30 per cent of every private health cover premium. Most health funds take the rebate directly off the premium though you can have it paid directly to you or claim it as part of your tax payment. Consequently there has been a large increase in the number of people taking out private health insurance and this, we would hope, will eventually lead to greater benefits.

The Federal Government has also removed the restrictions placed on health funds which stopped them from covering the expenses of a stay in hospital. This policy, referred to as 'no more gaps', means that your hospital bills will be covered by Medicare and your health fund. Of course, there are still doctors' fees and extras to be paid.

Lifetime health cover is another Federal Government initiative. It encourages you to join a health fund, which must include hospital cover. If you join before you turn 30 and keep it going, your premiums will be the lowest. The older you are on joining, the more it will cost. There is also a Medicare Surcharge: an extra 1 per cent if you earn over $50,000 (or $100,000 for a couple) and don't have a fund's hospital cover.

The Commonwealth Seniors Health Card (CSHC) is subject to an income test and is reviewed annually. It gives you all prescription medicines available through the Pharmaceutical Benefits Scheme (PBS) at a nominal cost. To obtain a CSHC you have to apply to Centrelink with copies of identification and your latest tax assessment. Once you have been accepted you must advise them of any change in your circumstances.

Bits & Bytes
Before travelling overseas talk to your health fund about the option to suspend your cover while you are away. This can be a worthwhile saving as the fund extends your membership by the number of weeks or months you are away. Your travel insurance covers you while out of the country.

SUPERANNUATION

Superannuation is a powerful way of accumulating wealth over time. It is the most widely discussed investment vehicle, because it increases national savings and encourages us to prepare for our own retirement. All super products have a taxation advantage over other forms of investment.

The Federal Government established the Superannuation Guarantee Fund on 1 July 1992. It is compulsory and tax effective — designed to accumulate capital to provide some income for retirement. If you are employed, a set percentage is taken out of your gross salary and you can add to this amount either directly or through your employer. If you are self-employed it is not compulsory to have your own fund but the Government encourages you with great tax concessions.

Keep track of your super — don't just hope that it's growing! You should know where it is invested, who the trustees are, what the investment strategy is, and what the earnings and charges are. Ask for regular statements so you know how it is growing. By being informed, you can adjust your other investments as you plan for your freedom years. Watch out for company failures in the super industry.

As a bumper sticker reminded us in 1992, the year of Super — Trust no one over five.

Bits and Bytes

There are now 7 taxpayers working for each retired person. By 2021 this figure will have dropped to 3.5. Think of how hard they will be working. We must increase our personal savings.

Superannuation must be thought of as a highly specialised form of investment. The tax on its income and capital gains is light, whereas all other investment income is taxed at the marginal rate. There are restrictions on when you have access to your money. It is locked up until you retire although there are exceptions. If you are suffering extreme hardship, you can appeal for its release. Check these conditions with the Trustee of your particular fund.

A super fund incurs ongoing management fees which, along with the tax payable, are deducted each year. You may think you have a $2,000 balance, but fees and tax will have reduced your investment. Don't forget there could be entrance and exit fees. The government has set a limit on fees payable by low-income earners. The rules change regularly!

Simply put, superannuation is an amount deducted regularly from income and put into a contributory super scheme which is invested to increase its value. A wide range of government and private funds is available, or you can set up your own. The fund structure consists of the following:

- The **members,** who contribute money and eventually become the beneficiaries.
- The **sponsors**, who arrange the establishment of the fund: e.g. employers, unions, companies, associations, governments, etc.
- The **trustees**, who administer the fund as set out in the Trust Deed and the *Superannuation Industry (Supervision) Act* 1993 (SIS) (Section 19). Investments are held in the trustees' names but the benefits belong to the members.
- The **fund managers**, nominated by the trustees to do the investing.
- The **regulators**, who check that the fund operates according to the legislation.

How much should you contribute? If you draw a wage the government has set the minimum that you and your employer must contribute. You can make additional payments, often referred to as topping up, but before committing yourself to extra payments, consider the implications on future social services benefits, accessibility and tax. Other investments may offer a better alternative, so seek advice on what to do with your extra savings.

How much will you get? Assuming an inflation rate of 4 per cent, a contribution of 9 per cent of salary and an investment earning rate of 7 per cent after tax and fees, the approximate lump sum you will receive will work out as follows:

Years	Times (X) your final salary
30	2.8
25	2.2
20	1.7
15	1.2
10	0.7
5	0.3

To know now how much that lump sum is actually going to be worth in real buying power when you receive it, work it out this way: if you contribute to a super fund for 30 years, the lump sum you receive then will buy you what 2.8 times your current salary would buy you now, so long as your salary remains constant and keeps pace with inflation. For example, if you earn $30,000 per year and you contribute to your super fund for 30 years, you should receive a lump-sum payment of $84,000 (which is $30,000 X 2.8).

With superannuation so liable to fluctuate, you may be excused for thinking that superannuation is not a reliable means of securing a comfortable retirement. Nevertheless, it offers good opportunities for tax savings and it provides a cornerstone for any investment plan.

Bits & Bytes
A woman can expect 25 years of retirement. These years are equal to a holiday of 1,300 weeks. Can you afford this holiday? Your super will take you part of the way, but you will have to help it along with your portfolio.

RETIREMENT SAVINGS ACCOUNT
The Retirement Savings Account (RSA) is a new type of passbook superannuation facility for self-employed, part-time and casual

workers. Small income-earners can pay in small amounts which of course earn only a low rate of interest. These accounts are safe and have much the same restrictions on access as super funds do.

Any financial institution providing an RSA must guarantee that you receive all contributions plus any interest credited to your account. They must notify you if your RSA goes above $10,000 to enable you to move to a higher income-producing super product.

Retirement

Once you have reached the age when you can withdraw your super (55 at present for most people) there are many options. These seem to alter every year, so you need to keep your finger on the pulse and a good working relationship with your financial adviser.

When you retire you are entitled to an Eligible Termination Payment (ETP) out of your super. You could roll over this money into an approved scheme or use a percentage to pay off loans such as your mortgage and purchase an approved annuity to give you a regular income. There are numerous rollover options available, all with different tax advantages. There are costs attached and advice is essential before making any decisions. These rules are complex and changing all the time.

An annuity is a contract with a financial institution to pay an income at regular intervals for a set period, in return for a lump sum. Each type has different taxation advantages and fees. It is also advisable to check the death benefits.

An immediate annuity enables you to exchange a lump sum from either your super or your savings, in return for a guaranteed regular income for an agreed period. At the end of the term you receive any remaining residual capital, but note that this amount can't exceed the original deposit. This is a fixed contract for both parties.

A lifetime annuity hedges your bets against outliving your money. You are paid an agreed sum, on agreed dates for the rest of your life. If you die before your money runs out — tough, nobody can inherit it. However, if you live longer than the amount you deposited you still receive the agreed income on the agreed dates for the rest of your life, as fixed in the contract.

An allocated annuity offers a regular allocated payment and can only be purchased with super or rollover money. You can vary the amount and frequency of payments, but you must take at least one distribution each year. Payments will not continue forever, they stop when your money runs out. Any money left in your account when you die becomes part of your estate, but, if your account runs out before you die, your income stops.

A deferred annuity lets you defer any payments until a specified date but it must start on your 65th birthday. At this point you can convert to another regular income product. It is closely tied to rollovers, and you need expert advice.

An allocated pension is basically the same as an allocated annuity, with a slightly different structure. It is a personal account from which you can draw regular payments, made up from either your rollover or super money. It offers flexibility but you can outlive your money. As with anything connected to rollovers or super, you need help from the experts before locking your money away.

Bits & Bytes

If you plan to live to a ripe old age, be aware that with allocated annuities and allocated pensions you run the risk of the money running out. The investment earnings that are going into the fund are keyed to the ups and downs of the market.

GENERAL PENSIONS

Centrelink is your first stop when you need financial help and have no resources. Find the nearest office listed in the phone book, and you will be advised on the vast range of resources available. Proof of identity and age are essential, so on your first visit take your birth certificate or passport with you.

Help is available from many sources, but pensions, like superannuation, keep changing. Some of them are:

Age If you think you are eligible for an age pension or part of one, your income and assets must be well documented. You do not need to include your home, but nearly everything else will be assessed by Centrelink. Exemptions for super payments are very complicated, so seek advice on them well before you retire.

Widows and divorcees Women over 50 may be eligible for an allowance but only if they were widowed, separated or divorced after turning 40.

Sole parents Centrelink will make sure you have enough resources to stay ahead and can help you get a part-time job, and then full employment. They can also help with education and training schemes when you are ready. They will also assist with childcare.

Carers Anyone caring for a disabled person may be able to claim this pension which also allows a respite period and time out to undertake further education or training.

Sickness and disability This type of pension is strictly controlled and requires medical approval. There is extra help for the blind or sight-impaired.

Unemployed Income support, job searching and student services are under constant review, and Centrelink can help in these fields. The youth allowance covers the 16–20 year olds and includes

AUSTUDY and unemployment allowances.

War veterans An extensive range of benefits is available for all veterans, their widows and dependants. These pensions do not have a means test. The Department of Veterans Affairs and, of course, the Returned and Services League of Australia (RSL) offer help and advice.

Remember that your home is exempt from the asset and income test. Selling it creates real problems unless you buy another home. Any capital gain can tip you over the limit when you are assessed for the pension. Ask your bank if it can offer a deeming account.

Deeming

Deem means to judge or consider, so the income test for pensions considers that you are earning a set amount on all investments before you are eligible for a pension. It applies to all recipients of a Centrelink or a Veterans' Affairs age pension.

Under this system all financial investments are assessed as earning a 'deemed' rate of interest for the income test. Most banks offer extended deeming accounts, which are available only to pensioners and some offer a two-tiered system of interest rates. Rates are set at the current deeming rate, or slightly higher if you can maintain more than around $30,000 in your account. This higher interest will not affect your pension, so go for it. Check how your bank views your savings, because they all differ on how they work out the percentage of interest paid.

Bits & Bytes
Don't trade a franked dividend income for the pension. If you sell your shares and put the proceeds into a low interest deposit to bring yourself under the income test to qualify for the pension, you could be much worse off in a couple of years. You have lost the capacity for capital growth. Seek expert advice.

14. FUN MONEY

• • •

Life is real! Life is earnest!
And the grave is not its goal.
Longfellow

All work and no play could drive you mad. While some of the activities in this chapter are way over the moon and not to be taken too seriously, allow yourself to dream that you might indulge in some of them. If you find you have some spare money after all that budgeting, saving and investing, you might like to consider some of these ideas for fun.

TRAVEL: THE WORLD IS YOUR OYSTER

It's time! Your investments are earning, your budget is working and travel is where our fun money goes! We read the travel sections of the newspapers avidly, especially the small advertisements. That is how we have chased bears in Hudson Bay, joined the Hopi Indians in their mesas, talked to the people of Murray Island early in the land rights debate, and white-water rafted through Murray Gates.

Planning for an overseas trip needs careful budgeting. If you are required to make a trip for work, take your holidays at the same time. If you are self-employed it is only a matter of organising your business. Airfares fluctuate, and there are seasonal fares, bargains for those booking well ahead and discounts for students and seniors. Always ask for a discount from your travel agent, especially if you are a regular client.

Women travelling alone face different attitudes and customs (especially dress rules) in foreign lands. Be well prepared for these before leaving home. The most important aspect of travelling alone is that you must be able to carry your own luggage in case there are long hikes and no porters at terminals.

Cards are best, east or west! A universally accepted credit card is the cheapest and safest way to carry money as you travel. A charge you make on your card is converted to Australian dollars when it reaches home at the exchange rate of that day. Arrange for your account to be paid before it becomes overdue and incurs interest or leave it in credit before flying out. A credit card is, without a doubt, the best way to go. A back up of travellers' cheques is wise for small expenses. Carry some local cash in small denominations for tipping, a taxi and a cup of coffee when you first arrive.

Keep track of every transaction on your card. It is easy to overspend.

Suppose you are in Rome and need local cash. Find an ATM compatible with your card, insert it, feed in your PIN. It talks to your bank at home via a central switching centre, it may go through two or three linked centres. Hey presto, 20 seconds later you have cash in the local currency in your hand. Remember, drawing cash on your card costs! There is also a 1 per cent currency conversion charge. Check exactly what your card covers before leaving home.

Avoid the transaction fees charged on travellers' cheques by hotels and banks by using a credit card. Another advantage of a card is if lost it can usually be replaced in a matter of hours. Travellers' cheques can also be replaced, providing you have safely recorded the numbers and report their loss immediately. Cash lost is gone forever.

Bits & Bytes
If you have chosen a four-letter PIN, learn it as a number because many overseas ATMs have only numeric keys or letters that do not correspond to ours.

Travel insurance is expensive but essential, never leave home without it. Make sure it includes medical cover, as this is vital. Travel insurance should also cover any loss, damage or theft of personal belongings, the cancellation of travel and personal liability. Shop around as there are big differences in costs and the cheapest cover is not always the best. Read the fine print. A tip for seniors: some companies charge extra for those aged 70, 75, or 80 while some will not insure you at all.

At any age, if you have an ongoing health problem, a doctor's certificate will be required. Overseas, the cost of medical assistance is incredibly high and it can be refused or delayed until you can prove your ability to pay. When travelling in Australia, your Medicare card takes care of any health problems.

If you're a bungy jumping or tow gliding enthusiast or take part in a riot or commit suicide, you are not covered by most travel insurance policies.

HOLIDAYS

Holidays need not involve expensive or extended travel. They are for fun and recharging your batteries.

Whether you long for a luxurious resort or a simple tent, a travel agent can find and book what you want. The Internet can now help you find the best place at the best price.

If you want economy, fun or somewhere to take the kids, a tent is cost-effective, and kids love camping. Tents are not just the basic sleep on the ground affairs — they can be very up-market with separate rooms and a verandah, but hiring is cheaper than buying unless you plan to camp a lot.

Another low-cost alternative is a caravan or campervan, either of which can be hired. Stationary caravans can be rented onsite at great holiday places. These are very popular, so book ahead.

During out-of-season holiday periods special deals are offered by resorts, cruise ships, hotels and motels, and camp sites. Some hotels include parking and theatre ticket specials and some interstate ones offer airfares too. How better to see the latest show than without the hassle of parking and driving home afterwards? The travel section of most newspapers and magazines will give you some ideas for the next holiday.

Organised tours are easy to book and usually economical. Good operators know the best places and the best value for your dollar, and they take care of all the details, leaving you to relax and enjoy your holiday. There are tours for a wide range of specific age groups and special interests.

Before you pay a deposit or the full amount for a tour or a flight, look into travel insurance that covers you if you or the agent cancels. Use a credit card that will build your frequent flyer points. After a couple of tours you may have enough points for a free flight.

PETS

From a mouse to a camel, they bring responsibility, companionship and great joy. Pets cost: they need feeding, they have expensive health services and need regular check-ups. Holidays can be a problem. If you take them with you make sure they will be accepted wherever you go. If you leave them behind you must organise and budget for their care by a kennel, cattery or carer. Veterinary health insurance is expensive but in most cases worthwhile.

DROPHEADS

A cabriolet used to mean a small two-wheeled horse-drawn carriage with two seats and a folding hood (from the Latin for a wild goat referring to 'lightness of movement'). It is now another name for a drophead coupe, a small car with a sunroof. Small, powerful and fun, its hood folds back and the wind takes over, making it nearly as exhilarating as a motorbike. It is expensive to buy, insure and keep on the road, very prone to theft (both as a whole or just for parts), but the joy!

> **Val** My husband and I decided to hire a car with a sunshine roof to tour Britain during what turned out

to be a rare and wonderful hot summer. We have never had an opening roof and we did not know there was a sunshield to pull over the glass. We cooked our way around the south of England until a local garage man clued us up. We both came home with a lovely English tan.

BOATS: 'I MUST GO DOWN TO THE SEA AGAIN'

Owning a boat means your hand is in your pocket forever, just like owning a horse. Even our small (two-women size) inflatable costs a lot, especially with an outboard motor and a full sailing kit, but the joy, the excitement and exercise are worth every cent to us.

> **Anne** I must be the only Sydneysider who was on the water, in the water and over the water of the harbour on Australia Day 1988. Yes, I fell in, wet rubber boats are slippery when the water is made so rough by the wake of thousands of boats. Then we flew over the Tall Ships, still in our wetsuits, covered by track suits — no time to change. This does show that for a small capital outlay you can have the joy of 'mucking about in boats'.

A canoe, an inflatable, a dinghy, a luxury yacht or whatever your purse can afford (not always what your heart desires) offer an escape for the young and the young at heart and for the fishing enthusiast, who can even supply dinner and save on the housekeeping. If you are a water person and don't want the responsibilities of owning or the fierce maintenance costs, hiring might suit your pocket and the occasion. Many boat sheds on lakes, rivers and harbours hire all types of boats, from runabouts to houseboats.

RACING: LEGS, WHEELS, WINGS AND WATER

Racing, whether by legs, wings, wheels or water, is a marvellous spectator sport. Horse racing is by far the most popular. Owning or part-owning a thoroughbred can be a bottomless pit for your fun money. The costs of buying, feeding, stabling, training and racing fees all need to be taken into account. Before you can race a horse you need a jockey. You might buy a winner but they are few and far between.

Owning a greyhound is not quite as expensive and if you train it yourself, you will be fit.

There's not much difference between watching pigeons and planes race. They both disappear and you are left with a stiff neck. The only way to enjoy planes is to fly your own. If you own a plane, you have already made your millions and don't need this book. Model planes are a cheaper way to go. Racing pigeons require a specialised knowledge of breeding and training, and travelling from meet to meet can take a lot of your time and your fun money.

Watching sailing races is not much better than watching pigeon unless you are on board and perpetually wet. Speed boats are noisy, smelly and exciting. All boats, whether speed, sailing or rowing are expensive to buy and keep in racing condition.

CASINOS

A small flutter is fun, a blow-out of the budget is disaster. The ambience of a casino encourages you to spend the housekeeping. It is so easy to be carried away, just like an auction when you come home with strange possessions and no money. Casinos put on great entertainment, so try watching the floor show instead of buying too many chips. If you must play the tables, limit your gambling money.

Bits and Bytes
The term blue chip, used to denote the top valued shares on the stock exchange, has its origin in big-time gambling. The highest valued gaming chip used by casinos is the blue one.

'FRIENDS'

Organisations of all sorts — from art galleries to philatelic clubs — have friends. In return for supporting them with your subscription, you gain entree to a whole range of activities at a nominal cost, and increase your circle of friends with similar interests.

SHOPPING

Harrods and Saks here we come, loaded with credit cards and the occasional roll of dollars in case there is an extra discount for cash.

You can now take a special shoppers' flight to Los Angeles just to visit its many discount price clubs and reject stores. Local bus companies also organise tours around the factory outlet circuit. This has become a great money-spinner for the charities that run them as they get a percentage of all proceeds. The range of factories with seconds shops has grown and now covers everything imaginable.

SPORT

As a babe in arms we are pointed down this track whether we like it or not. Those of us who do enjoy sport progress from school teams to fitness classes and then to our dream — sailing the Caribbean or skiing the slopes of Mont Blanc.

Your sporting activities need not cost a fortune — join a club, tennis, golf or fitness. Remember to include these ongoing costs in your budget plan, and think of what it is doing for your health and figure!

Bits & Bytes
How to open a Swiss bank account.
To begin with you need a million dollars and an introduction, so get out there and meet the right people! You also need to know the bank and the type of account you want. Then you will need the bank's approval — it won't touch you if you

look like a Godmother. An Austrian bank account is now considered as discreet and safe, but it does not have the same panache as a Swiss bank account.

It's your fun money. Enjoy spending it — we do:

Wall-to-wall whales. Mothers with calves, young bachelors, experienced males anxious to mate (as a point of interest its 'equipment' is 8 feet long and pink carrying 2,000 pounds of sperm) and with us in the middle — eight of us in a Zodiac Inflatable.

This was the day for which we had flown half-way round the world: our first eye-to-eye contact with the Californian grey whales at Boca de Soledad in Magdalena Bay, Baja. And those eyes — 'Just like a jersey cow's, brown, deep and so friendly.'

Then it happened. A mother and calf played with us, under the boat, alongside, slowly turning to inspect us. Mother allowed herself to be touched, her skin soft and spongy, like a de-haired pig or a well-set jelly with barnacles firmly attached that were lethal to our loving hands. Anne, safely wedged in the stern, could only watch as everyone else almost fell over the side reaching out to feel this giant mammal of the sea. Then, over the transom, came a small calf to commune with Anne. As one of our travelling companions described her feelings later at that night's recap, 'It's the closest I have been to understanding my place in the universe.'

CONTACTS

• • •

Questions, worries, complaints — all arise in every field at some time in our lives. Some problems can be fixed quickly and easily if we know where to turn. The following organisations and associations offer help and advice.

Addresses and telephone numbers may change, so check your phone book first. Phone calls from anywhere in Australia to numbers with the prefix 13 are only charged at local call rates. The STD code is not needed. The local, state and commonwealth governments entries in the front pages of the phone book are marvellous sources of information. It's worth a browse.

Newspapers carry a financial section which will keep you informed of daily movements in the markets, even farm produce, interest and exchange rates. *The Financial Review*, also a daily, gives a far more detailed account — for when you are a big time trader. Specialist magazines, (monthly or quarterly) will keep you up to date with the market. They also list the value of trusts, bonds, super, allocated pensions and annuities.

Association of Independent Retirees This is a growing association with branches in cities and regional areas.
1800 777 324

Association of Superannuation Funds of Australia (ASFA) It represents most of Australia's super funds and offers consumer information on the various funds, including self-managed funds.
1800 812 798
www.superannuation.asn.au

Australian Banking Industry Ombudsman (ABIO) Set up by the banking industry, it handles any complaints or disputes you may

have with your bank. It is a free service and has the authority to make awards.
1800 337 444

Australian Competition and Consumer Commission (ACCC) This Commonwealth Government body wields a lot of clout. It looks into complaints against businesses that have stretched or broken the law. It does not deal, however, with specific consumer complaints.
1300 302 502
www.accc.gov.au

Australian Consumers' Association (ACA) Founded in 1959, it provides information and advice on goods, services, health and finance. It publishes CHOICE magazine, which makes expert assessments of consumer items, testing and rating them on quality, safety and price. The ACA also publishes a wide range of informative, easy to understand books on all facets of daily living. It is an independent body funded by its magazine subscriptions and sales. It actively lobbies all government bodies.
(02) 9577 3333
www.choice.com.au

Australian Investors' Association (AIA) This is an association for individual investors who run discussion courses for interested investors.
1300 555 061
www.investors.asn.au.

Australian Prudential Regulation Authority (APRA) This is a government body is the one to approach if you are suffering financial hardship in relation to your super payments.
131 060
www.apra.gov.au

Australian Securities and Investments Commission (ASIC) As the government's corporate watchdog, makes sure that prospectuses for share floats or unit trusts follow the rules set out for such publication. It also keeps track of fees and commissions being charged and disclosed. Its Infoline will advise you on choosing a financial adviser, superannuation problems, shareholders' rights at AGMs and changes to corporate law. It produces many excellent booklets.
1300 300 630
www.asic.gov.au

Australian Shareholders' Association (ASA) This nationwide group, formed by volunteers to help the small investor, has grown dramatically over the last few years. It is now able to put pressure on listed companies to be more accountable and to be more aware of their small shareholders.
1300 368 448
www.asa.asn.au

Australian Stock Exchange (ASX) It has an office in each capital city. Most run excellent courses for new investors starting in the market and for experienced traders wishing to learn more. You can take a home course, for a fee, which includes comprehensive reference notes along with exercises. Or you can phone the ASX customer service line with a query.
1300 300 279
www.asx.com.au

Australian Taxation Office (ATO) Its excellent free booklets cover all areas of the tax system and are up-dated whenever the rules change. It has offices in all states and many suburbs, but some offer over-the-counter limited advice. Phone for help on:
Personal tax info 13 2863
Private health, Medicare levy 13 2862
HECS, family tax assistance 132861

Superannuation helpline 13 1020
Reasonable benefits limits 13 2864
Problem resolution/complaints 13 2870

The ATO's 24-hour, 7-day fax service will advise you on personal tax, super, HECS and business tax.
132 860
www.ato.gov.au

Automobile Associations are in every state and their services include road service, accommodation lists, mechanical inspections and financial services.

Centrelink It links all Australian government services, such as employment, pensions, health and student allowances. Your phone book lists your closest office.
www.centrelink.gov.au

Chartered Accountants in Australia The national office in Sydney will answer your questions.
(02) 9290 1344
www.icaa.org.au

Council on the Aging (COTA) Branches in all capital cities are listed in the local phone book.

Credit Advantage Limited Contact this office if you need access to your records of credit.
(02) 9464 6000
www.creditadvantage.com.au

Credit Union Dispute Resolution Centre Its name is self-explanatory.
1800 624 241

CONTACTS

Fair Trading Offices in each state and territory help solve a wide range of consumer problems. Check your phone book and State government website — (e.g. www.nsw.gov.au).

Family Law Legal Advice Ring them for help in dealing with any family separation problems.
1800 632 930

Financial Industry Complaints Services (FICS) Set in place to assist superannuation or life insurance policyholders, or those who have products sold by licensed security dealers or fund managers.
1800 335 405
www.fics.asn.au

Financial Planning Association of Australia (FPA) Ask them for a list of their members if you need advice on finding a financial adviser, if you need to check on your chosen adviser's conduct or qualifications, or if you are unhappy with the service you are receiving.
1800 626 393
www.fpa.asn.au

Financial Services Complaints Resolutions Scheme Set up to receive complaints about the behaviour of any FPA members.
1800 670 040

Franchise Council of Australia Not yet in all states but head office can be contacted for advice.
(03) 9650 1667
www.fca.com.au

Insurance Enquiries and Complaints An organisation that deals with consumer complaints about general insurance and provides information on any general insurance matter.
1300 363 683
www.iecltd.com.au

Law Society Each state has its own Law Society to advise you about choosing a solicitor. In country areas local councils should be able to help with this.

National Information Centre on Retirement Investments (NICRI) A free, independent and confidential service that aims to extend the information available for all small investors planning for their retirement or facing redundancy. It has excellent free pamphlets.
1800 020 110
www.nicri.org.au

Ombudsman Each state (and the Commonwealth) has its own department to deal with any kind of complaint (see the next entry). Check your phone book.

Private Health Insurance Ombudsman This is the department to consult over any private health insurance problems.
1800 640 695
www.phio.org.au

Real Estate Institutes Offices in each state will give any help required.

Securities Institute of Australia If you want to turn your investment interest into a career, or just expand your knowledge, ask the Securities Institute. They offer accredited postgraduate and open-entry level courses.
(02) 9251 6799
www.securities.edu.au

Seniors cards Each state issues its own card. To apply, phone your state office.
1300 364 758
www.seniorscard.nsw.gov.au

Small Business Association of Australia Here's a good place to start if you're planning to set up your own business.
(02) 9819 7208

Superannuation Complaints Tribunal (SCT) This statutory authority resolves complaints about superannuation, annuities and related subjects.
131 434
www.sct.gov.au

Volunteering Australia It coordinates all those people with time and a wish to help others.
(03) 9663 6994
www.volunteeringaustralia.org.au

GLOSSARY

• • •

Bear market: a second-hand store for stuffed grizzlies?
Odd lot: a parking garage for peculiar cars?

ALL ORDINARIES INDEX The measure of price movement of the overall share market. It is calculated each day using the current price of the top 500 Australian companies listed on the Australian Stock Exchange.

ANNUITY A regular payment made in exchange for a lump sum. Payments are set at the purchase time, can be for life, for a set period, or indexed for inflation. This useful income stream can now be attached to a super payout.

ASSET Anything you own that is valuable or useful. Net assets are what remain after your total liabilities have been subtracted from your total assets.

AT CALL Money invested in the market for example, or interest calculated daily that can be withdrawn any time by 'calling' for it.

AT DISCRETION A client may instruct his or her stockbroker to buy or sell at a price left up to the broker's discretion.

AT MARKET An order to buy or sell shares at the market price at the time that the order is given.

BANKRUPT People are declared bankrupt by the courts when their debts exceed their assets and their creditors can't be paid.

BEAR MARKET A falling market.

BENEFICIARY A person who gains a benefit — usually referring to an amount or asset bequeathed by a will.

BLUE CHIP Applied to shares, usually high-priced, in a company that reliably turns in a profit in good times or bad.

BOND An IOU from a government or corporation as a promise to pay interest in return for the use of money, usually a secure investment.

GLOSSARY

BONUS ISSUE The issue of bonus or free shares to existing stockholders.

BOURSE Another name for a stock exchange of French origin.

BULL MARKET A market in which the prices are rising.

CAPITAL The value of your assets.

CAPITAL GAIN The profit made from the sale of an asset, such as shares or property. It is the difference between the amount you paid for an item and the amount you received on its sale.

CAPITAL GAINS TAX A tax levied on capital gains on assets acquired after 20 September 1985. Your home is exempt.

CASH MANAGEMENT TRUST A managed investment option in the short-term money markets.

CHESS (Clearing House Electronic Subregister System) An electronic transfer and settlement system operated by the ASX.

COMPOUND INTEREST Interest that is not drawn but added to the capital to increase earnings.

CONSUMER PRICE INDEX (CPI) Measures the changes in the price of a 'basket' of goods and services that is issued quarterly.

CONTRACT NOTE A document sent to a buyer or seller listing details of the transaction.

CONTRIBUTING SHARE A share that is not fully paid.

CONVERTIBLE NOTE A loan at a fixed rate of interest for a fixed term which can be redeemed for cash or shares on maturity.

DEAD HEADS A term referring to investments, especially shares, not living up to expectations.

DEBENTURE A secured loan made to a company at a fixed term.

DEED In law it is a signed, sealed and delivered document to ratify the transfer or conveyance of property.

DIVIDEND The amount of a company's net profits that is paid to its shareholders, usually every six months.

DIVIDEND IMPUTATION The tax credit attached to franked dividends.

EARNINGS PER SHARE (EPS) A company's net profit divided by the total number of shares in the company; usually expressed as cents per share.

183

ECONOMY The management of the resources of a business or country.

ELIGIBLE TERMINATION PAYMENT (ETP) Part of the payments received on retirement, retrenchment or resignation or if you draw money out of super. It has tax advantages.

EQUITY In the share market *equities* are ordinary shares in a company's assets as distinct from debt securities such as bonds and debentures.

EX (or ex-dividend) indicates that the shares are being traded without the current dividend, which is retained by the seller.

EXCHANGE RATE The value of one country's currency compared to that of another.

FACE VALUE The amount at which securities are issued, stated on the document.

FIXED INTEREST Interest set at a specific rate for an agreed period.

FLOAT The initial raising of capital, to be used to 'float' a company in the market, obtained by public subscription.

FRANKED DIVIDEND Tax has been paid at company rates giving the shareholder a tax credit. A partially franked dividend has a lower rate of tax paid.

FRONT END FEES The upfront fees payable on entering a financial contract.

GEARING Borrowing to invest.

GOODWILL An invisible asset created by a good reputation for work well done.

GREENBACK The US dollar.

GROSS DOMESTIC PRODUCT (GDP) The measurement of the flow of goods and services within the country

GROWTH STOCK Stock with good prospects for future expansion, promising capital gain.

HEDGING Taking steps to reduce the risk of financial loss on an investment, mostly in the futures market.

HOLDER IDENTIFICATION NUMBER (HIN) Allocated by your stockbrokers when you nominate them as your sponsor in CHESS.

INDEXED The value of an asset that has increased, usually in line with the CPI.

INFLATION A progressive increase in the level of prices when money loses value.

INSIDER TRADING Gaining profit by trading in shares with knowledge that was not available to the market. An unlawful practice.

INTESTATE Dying without having left a will.

INVESTOR A person who outlays capital in an enterprise expecting a profit in return for the use of the money.

LIABILITY or debt. Both terms mean how much a company, or person, owes; the opposite of asset.

LIQUIDATOR A person appointed to take charge of a company when it is wound up.

LIQUIDITY The measure of how easily assets can be converted into cash.

LISTED A company or trust whose shares are listed on the exchange for trading.

MANAGED INVESTMENTS Professionally managed funds that pool moneys of numerous investors to their mutual advantage.

MARKET PRICE The price to buy or sell shares and securities on the open market.

MANAGEMENT EXPENSE RATIO (MER) The percentage of a managed fund's balance needed to cover fees and charges.

MERCHANT BANK A specialist bank that trades in money, securities and the futures market rather than using its own funds to arrange finance between various institutions.

MORTGAGE A document or deed of promise to repay a loan, using property as security.

MORTGAGEE The party who lends money on the security of property.

MORTGAGOR The party who receives the loan with their property as security.

MUTUAL FUND A group of investors pooling money in specialised areas such as motoring organisations.

NEGATIVE GEARING Occurs when an investment produces less income than the interest being paid on the borrowed funds

NOMINAL INTEREST, or simple interest Paid at a flat rate at the end of an agreed term.

NOMINAL VALUE The value of an asset before taking into account income.

OMBUDSMAN A person who investigates any complaints against the state or federal government or an organisation. The banking and private health insurance industries have each appointed their own ombudsman.

OPTION The right to take up property or shares on specific terms within or at a set time.

ORDINARY SHARES The most commonly traded shares. They are fully-paid shares but earn lower dividends than debentures and preference shares do. Ordinary shareholders have voting rights and can attend AGMs.

PAR VALUE The nominal value of a security. The par value of a share is set at issue and is the face value of the share, which can be quite different to its market price.

PER ANNUM (PA) Every year or by the year.

PORTFOLIO A collection of different types of investments. A wise investor builds a balanced portfolio based on personal needs and future requirements. The prime investments are usually shares or equities and real estate.

PREFERENCE SHARES Can have a fixed dividend rate and limited voting rights. Their dividends rank above ordinary shares but below debentures.

PROFIT The money gained after all expenses have been paid.

PROSPECTUS The document that sets out the terms of a new issue of investments, shares or securities offered to the public. It must conform to the rules of the ASX and the ASIC.

PROXY The written authorisation given to a person to act on behalf of another: extensively used at company AGMs when a shareholder is unable to attend.

PUBLIC SECTOR The area of the economy controlled by state and Commonwealth governments.

RATE OF RETURN The return on capital invested, usually expressed as a percentage.

REAL VALUE or real terms These take inflation into account when calculating value.

REBATE A reduction in the amount of a payment due.

RECESSION A time of slow or stagnant economic activity and productivity, rising unemployment, and lower interest rates. Not as severe as a depression.

RETAINED EARNINGS — Profits retained after paying dividends and expenses, they appear in the balance sheet

R & M Repairs and maintenance, a short form commonly used by the building and motor trades.

RIGHTS ISSUE An offer to shareholders to buy new shares, usually at a price lower than market price.

ROLLOVER A fund that complies with the Government's rules for a continuation of your super on changing jobs or after retirement. You are deferring the tax that would be due if you withdrew money from your fund or ETP.

SCRIPT A numbered document that identifies the person as the registered holder of shares or securities. Under the ASX CHESS program, share scripts are becoming a thing of the past.

SEATS (Stock Exchange Automated Trading System) Has taken share trading from the floor of the stock exchange to the screens in traders' offices.

SECURITISATION Mortgages are bundled together to give security of the strength of numbers, thereby reducing interest rates for the borrower.

SECURITIES The various types of investment, such as shares, debentures and bonds, offered by a company or government body.

SECURITY REFERENCE NUMBER (SRN) Allocated to you when you buy shares in a company and you retain the company as your sponsor. It is an alternative to HIN when you choose to be sponsored by a broker.

SHARE An equity part ownership in a company. (See also *equity*.)

SIMPLE INTEREST Interest calculated on money invested for an agreed period.

STAG A buyer of new share issues who sells on the first day of trading in attempt to make a quick profit.

STALE CHEQUE According to the Cheques & Payments Orders Act of 1986, after 15 months a bank has no authority to honour a cheque.

STOCKBROKER A Stock Exchange Member who buys and sells stocks, shares and securities for clients.

SUPERANNUATION A savings plan, not unlike life insurance, which is invested in public and private sector schemes. Contributions are made by both the employee and employer and are taxed at a low rate. It is designed to help fund the retirement needs of the population and is in a constant state of change.

TAXATION The compulsory contribution to the expenses of public administration imposed by government.

TRUST Commercially speaking, a trust is a pool of invested assets operating for the benefit of all members; formed by the issue of a legal document — the Trust Deed. A trust enables small investors access to a wide range of investments.

TRUSTEE The party appointed to supervise the operations of the investment of assets held by the trust and to invest for the mutual benefit of the members.

UNDERWRITER Arranges a new issue of shares or securities and agrees to purchase any that are unsold to guarantee a full subscription.

YIELD The annual return on an investment, given as a percentage of current market value.

INDEX

● ● ●

10 per cent rule 15, 27
52-week high/low 92

accountants 59, 110
accounts 41–2
  deeming 166
  joint 137
  passbook 46
  advice, expert 19,
    55–60
  age pension 18, 19,
    23, 165, 166
All Ordinaries Index (All
  Ords) 80, 81, 92
allocated pension 164
annuities 163–4
assets 18, 25–6
  diminishing 25
  intangible 25, 119
  tangible 95
ATMs (automatic teller
  machines) 40, 44
auctions
  car 150
  real estate 101–2, 113
Australian Business
  Number (ABN) 129
Australian Financial
  Institutions
  Commission 40
Australian Securities and
  Investments
  Commission (ASIC)
  55–6, 59, 80, 81
Australian Stock
  Exchange (ASX)
  55–6, 57, 79–81
  courses 94
  industrial shares 84
  Investor Hours 94
  mining/oil shares 84

Open Day 94
SEATS 80, 87
  tracking shares 92–3
Australian Taxation
  Office (ATO) 130–1

balloon payment 35
bank bills 52, 70
banking 39–41
  accounts 41–2
  charges 46, 47
  deposits 45
  electronic 44, 48
  fee reduction 47
  financial advice 59, 89
  identification 42–3
  by phone 44
  statements 46
  withdrawals 45
Banking Act 39, 40
bankruptcy 35–6, 37
banks 39, 40, 47, 48, 59
  see also banking
bill paying 45
  direct debit 41
blue chip shares 52, 54,
    83, 172
boats 151, 171, 172
borrowing 29–30, 35,
    36, 97
  gearing 55, 62, 107,
    110
  interest 60–1
bridging finance 105
brokers *see* stockbrokers
budgeting 14, 17, 26–8,
    97, 155, 158
building inspection 99
building insurance 144
building societies 39
bulk buying 147

business
buying 119–21
  establishment costs
    122–4
  setting up 118–19
Business Activity
  Statement (BAS) 123
buybacks 82
buying power 162

capital gain 62
Capital Gains Tax 75,
    86, 87, 89, 91,
    112–13, 128, 131–3,
    136–7
  home exempt 95, 98,
    117–18
  on real estate 112–13
capital growth 51, 52,
    60–1, 77, 79, 81
capital guarantee 50
capital loss 18
car racing 172
cars 26
  buying new 149
  buying second-hand
    150–1
  costs 144–5
  dropheads 170
  leasing 145
  maintenance 152
cash management trusts
    53, 69
casinos 172
Centrelink 165
charge cards 33
cheques 41, 45–6
CHESS (Clearing House
  Electronic Subregister
  System) 82, 87, 88–9
childcare 142–3

189

children 15, 16, 51–2
costs 142–3, 145–7
    education 146
    investing for 146–7
    school holidays 148
clothes, for work 142
clubs 148
collectables 59, 74–5
    traders in 59
Commonwealth Seniors Health Card 19, 159
companies
    limited 121
    no liability 121–2
    proprietary 121
company tax 128
Company Title 107
computer costs 117
consultancy 116
Consumer Price Index (CPI) 63
contents insurance 144
contract notes 87
contributing shares 85
convertible notes 85
conveyancing 99–100
Corporations Law 55, 58, 80
cost cutting 141–8
coupon payments 69–70
credit 29–31
Credit Advantage 35
credit cards 31, 36, 41, 45
    for travel 167–8, 170
credit insurance 30
credit rating 35
credit unions 39–40
customs duty 128

DAX index 93
debentures 69
debit cards 31, 32
debt 30–1, 36–7
deeming 166
depreciation 110–11, 144
depressions 50
direct debit 41

direct selling 124
disability insurance 157
disability pension 165
discount brokers 57
diversification 83
dividend imputation 82, 90–1
Dividend Reinvestment Plan (DRP) 86
dividends 43, 52, 79, 82
    franking 55, 62, 82, 90, 92, 166
dollar cost averaging 61–2
domestic help 142, 156
Dow Jones index 93

education/training 124–5
EFTPOS 40, 44, 45
electronic banking 44
Eligible Termination Payment 163
emergencies 53, 81
entertaining, at home 148
excise duty 128
exercise 147

face value 63
factory outlets 147, 173
financial
    advisers/planners 55–7, 59, 89
    State of Advice (SOA) 56
Financial Planning Association of Australia (FPA) 55–6
Financial Transaction Reports Act 42
fingerscanning 34
floats 86
franchises 120–1
franking *see* dividend imputation
Frog Focus 88
FTSE 100 index 93
fund managers 58

futures 86

gearing 62
    see also negative gearing
goals 66–7
Goods and Services Tax (GST) 123, 127, 128–9
goodwill 119
government bonds 69–70
grossed up yield 93
guarantor, acting as 36
Guide to Capital Gains Tax 133

hardware stores 153
health insurance 19, 54, 147, 158–9
heritage property 112
hire purchase 34
holidays 169–70
home 18, 26, 95, 97, 166
    and CGT 95, 98, 117–18
    cost cutting 143–4
    entertaining 148
    equity 17, 19, 25
    repairs/maintenance 111–12
    sale-lease-back 19
    see also mortgages
home loans 42, 49, 61, 103–6
home office 116–18
horse racing 171
housing loans *see* home loans

imputation credits 90–1
income, from shares 53, 68, 77
income tax 128, 129–30
inflation 54, 63
insider trading 81
insurance 54, 122, 147, 155–9
    brokers/agents 155

INDEX

building 144
business expense 122
contents 144
  disability 157
  general 156
  health 158–9
  life 157–8
  pets 156, 170
  trauma 157–8
  travel 168–70
interest 43, 60–1
  compound 60–1, 69
  simple 60
interest rate 61, 63
interest-bearing deposits 67–8
Internet
  banking 44, 48
  share trading 57–8, 88
investment 16, 17–18, 21–5, 49, 65–6
  dollar cost averaging 61–2
inflation 54, 63
  leverage 62
  options 67–75
  risk 50, 52, 53, 54–5, 65
  tracking 75
see also income; interest
Investment Clock 49–50
Investment Club 90
investment planning 51–4
  accumulation 54
  diversification 54
  expert advice 55–60
  growth 53
  quality 54, 84
  research 24–5, 55
  tax 55
investment properties 107–11

joint accounts 137

land tax 111, 128
lawyers 58

lay-by 34
leverage 62
liabilities 25
life insurance 157–8
limited company 121
loans see borrowing; home loans

managed funds 70–3
money, and relationships 138–9
money management 13–19, 22, 24–5, 65–6
mortgages 61, 96, 97, 98, 103–6, 108
  early payout 105
  insurance 100, 144
motorbikes 151

National Guarantee Fund (NGF) 58
negative gearing 55, 62, 107, 110
Nikkei index 93
no liability company 121–2

outsourcing 115, 116
overdrafts 30, 41

P/E ratio 93
passbook accounts 46
PAYG (pay as you go) tax 123, 128, 130
pensions 165–6
  age 18, 19, 23, 165, 166
  allocated 164
  carer 165
  sickness/disability 165
  sole parent 165
  unemployed 165–6
  war veteran 166
  widow/divorcee 165
pets 156, 170
phone banking 44
phonecards 33
pigeon racing 172

PIN (personal identification number) 44, 168
planes 151–2, 172
portfolios
  assessing share performance 91–3
  balanced 83
  ready-made 93–4
power of attorney 134–5
preference shares 85
Privacy Act 35
property
  buying off the plan 102–3
proof of ownership 106–7
  titles 106–7
see also real estate
property auctions 101–2, 113
property syndicates 73
property trusts 72–3, 96
proprietary company 121
purchasing power 63

racing 171–2
rates 101, 128
ready-made portfolios 93–4
real estate 15, 22, 25, 52–3, 54, 95–7
  agents/valuers 59
renting 97–8, 143
research 98
  selling 112–13
real estate, buying 98–9
  agent/private 102
  at auction 101–2
  building inspections 99
  conveyancing 99–100
  costs 99–101
  establishment fee 100
  insurance 100
  off the plan 102–3
  option to purchase 100

191

proof of ownership 106–7
rates 101, 128
repairs/maintenance 111–12
record keeping 46, 75, 89, 91, 111, 132–3
redundancy 115–16
relationships, and money 138–9
rent and buy plans 35
renting *see* real estate
Reserve Bank 39, 63
retirement 13, 16, 17, 18, 23–4, 67, 162
Retirement Savings Account 162–3
retrenchment 115–16
rule of 72 37

saving 15, 26, 96
 10 per cent rule 15, 27
school holidays 148
SEATS (Stock Exchange Automated Trading System) 80, 87
seconds shops 147, 173
securitisation 105–6
self-funded retirees 61
Seniors Health Card 19, 159
share funds 72
shares 14–15, 17, 22–3, 73, 77–9, 83
 advantages 81–3
 assessing performance 91–3
 blue chip 52, 54, 83, 172
 bonus issue 79, 85
 buybacks 82
 buying/selling 86–8
 contributing 85
 convertible notes 85
 floats 86
 fringe benefits 83
 futures/options 86
 guidelines 83–4
 loan security 82
 new issues 82
 ordinary 84–5
 preference 85
 rights issue 79, 82, 85
 takeovers 86
 tracking 89
shopping 173
small business *see* business
smart cards 33, 44
solicitors 58
sport 148, 173
stock market 77, 78–9, 84, 90, 93
 Bulls and Bears 89
stockbrokers 57–8, 79, 81, 86–7
store cards 31, 32
stored value cards 31, 33, 44
Strata Title 106–7, 156
superannuation 13, 15, 62–3, 67, 160–2
 complicated 18–19, 122–3, 130
 withdrawing 163–4
Superannuation Guarantee Fund 23, 62, 160

tax audit 131
tax file number 43, 92
Tax Pack 129–30
taxation 55, 68, 90–1, 111, 127–33
 in business 123, 127–9
telecommuting 116–18, 143
term deposits 52, 53, 68–9
term life insurance 157
Torrens Title 106
tradesmen 153
Training Guarantee Levy 123
trauma insurance 157–8
travel 167–9
 insurance 168–70

unemployment 37, 165–6
unit trusts 70–3
unsecured notes 69

warehouse outlets 147, 173
wealth 21–2
wills (legal) 54, 135–7
 intestacy 136